DATE DUE

DATE DUE			
OCT 3 1 1995			
DEC 1 8 1996			
MAR 0 7 1997			
MAR 2 6 1998			
SE 2 9 98			
DEC 0 1 1999			
Fac 99-00			
GAYLORD			PRINTED IN U.S.A.

CULTURES OF THE WORLD

CHILE

Jane Kohen Winter

MARSHALL CAVENDISH
New York • London • Sydney

Reference edition published 1992 by
Marshall Cavendish Corporation
2415 Jerusalem Avenue
North Bellmore
New York 11710

Editorial Director	Shirley Hew
Managing Editor	Shova Loh
Editors	Roseline Lum
	Siow Peng Han
	Leonard Lau
	MaryLee Knowlton
Picture Editor	Jane Duff
Production	Edmund Lam
Design	Tuck Loong
	Lee Woon Hong
	Dani Phoa
	Ong Su Ping
	Katherine Tan
Illustrator	Thomas Koh

Printed in Singapore

Library of Congress Cataloging-in-Publication Data:
Winter, Jane Kohen, 1959–
        Chile / Jane Kohen Winter.
          p. cm.—(Cultures Of The World)
        Includes bibliographical references and index.
        Summary: Introduces the history, geography,
           culture, and lifestyles of Chile.
        ISBN 1 85435 522 8
        1. Chile. [1. Chile.] I. Title. II. Series.
F3058.5.W56 1991
983—dc20   90-22472
                                    CIP
                                    AC

INTRODUCTION

CHILE is a land of exquisite natural beauty and a unique geography. The north is dominated by the Atacama Desert, some regions of which have never had a single drop of rain. The Central Valley is known for its perfect climate and fertile soil, and the southern region for its fierce winds, icy temperatures, rough seas and terrific storms. The country's western border is the Pacific Ocean, which provides Chile with an amazing range of seafood, and its eastern border is the stunning Andean mountain range.

The Chilean people share a common language, religion and ethnic background. Educated, artistic and cosmopolitan, Chileans are also thought to be some of the friendliest, most open-minded people in Latin America.

This book, part of the *Cultures of the World* series, provides insight into the Chilean lifestyle: how Chileans think, how they live, what they eat, and how they spend their leisure time.

Santiago

CONTENTS

Ranger at Paine National Park in southern Chile, one of South America's newest nature reserves.

CONTENTS

Cures on wheels offered by a folk medicine seller.

GEOGRAPHY

GEOGRAPHICALLY, CHILE is certainly one of South America's most unusual countries. The longest narrow country in the world, Chile stretches 2,650 miles from north to south on the Pacific coast, but the average width is only 110 miles. The Atacama Desert shields Chile from Peru, its neighbor to the north, just as the Andes, which cover a third of its total area, separate it from Argentina and Bolivia, both to the east. With an area of more than 302,000 square miles, Chile is almost twice the size of California, a bit larger than Texas, and about the size of France.

Where the country got its name remains a mystery. Some believe that "Chile" derives from a Peruvian Indian word that means "cold." Others say it comes from another Indian language and means "land's end." A third group believes it derives from the call of a bird, "cheele-cheele."

Chile is unstable, meteorologically as well as geologically. Flash floods caused by the rapid melting of snow in the Andes damage villages regularly. Fishermen are always on the alert for sudden storms and strong currents. More than 100 earthquakes have been recorded since 1575, most of them in the south. These are often followed by tremendous tidal waves. Major cities such as Valparaíso and Concepción have been damaged repeatedly by natural disasters.

The terrain ranges from exceedingly dry desert in the north, to green Central Valley, to heavily forested Lake District in the south, to icy fjords and glaciers at the southernmost tip. Because of Chile's great length, daylight hours vary greatly. On the longest day of the year, Arica (north), gets about 13 hours' daylight, while Puerto Williams (far south), gets 17.

Opposite: **A candelabrum cactus, one of the few plants that will grow in the Atacama Desert in northern Chile.**

Desert blooms peek through crevices in the hardened mud slabs in the Atacama Desert after rain.

NORTH, MIDDLE AND SOUTH CHILE

Chile can be divided into three major geographic regions which differ dramatically in terms of population, climate, topography and natural resources. North Chile, which ranges from the Peruvian border to the city of La Serena, includes the bleak, thinly populated Atacama Desert, some areas of which have never had a single drop of rain. North Chile contains great deposits of nitrates and copper, which make an important contribution to the nation's economy.

Middle Chile contains what is known as the Central Valley, the country's heartland, which stretches 600 miles from the Aconcagua River in the north to Puerto Montt in the south. Some 80% of the population lives in the major cities of this region, which is said to bear a striking resemblance to the central valley of California: Santiago (population 5 million), the capital of Chile; Valparaíso (population 275,000), Chile's major port; and Concepción (population 280,000). The central region is green and highly cultivated. Snow-capped Andean peaks with some of the world's best skiing resorts are only a few hours' drive from Santiago, and the beach resort of Viña del Mar is only a three-hour drive to the west.

The Central Valley is traversed by the Maipo, Maule, Itata and Bío-Bío rivers. South of the Bío-Bío lies Chile's Lake District, which has been likened to the Pacific Northwest of the United States in terms of climate, and Switzerland in terms of scenic grandeur. In Villarrica, a major resort town, an active volcano occasionally pours white-hot lava over its snow-capped peaks, a most unusual sight. The area contains deep-blue lakes, stunning glaciers and lush forests and is a prime vacation spot for Chileans.

Chile's Lake District is characterized by such topographical features as the 8,809-foot Volcan Villarrica. The volcano rises high above the major resort town of Villarrica and occasionally spews white-hot lava.

"The sense of sublimity, which the ... forest-clad mountains of Tierra del Fuego excited in me ... has left an indelible impression on my mind."

— Charles Darwin, in "Voyage of the Beagle"

Many of Chile's German immigrants and most of the remaining native Indians of Chile, the Mapuche, live in the Lake District.

South Chile extends from Chiloé Island to Cape Horn, South America's southernmost point, and contains a maze of hundreds of small islands, dramatic fjords, and glaciers. Punta Arenas, the most southerly city, lies on the Magellan Strait, an important passageway from the Atlantic to the Pacific before the opening of the Panama Canal in 1914. Across the strait lies the Tierra del Fuego or "Island of Fire," which is shared with Argentina.

South Chile has violent climatic conditions with terrific storms, freezing rains and high winds. Although South Chile occupies one-third of the country's land area, it is populated by a small percentage of its people.

Right: **In the days before the opening of the Panama Canal, seafarers, including Ferdinand Magellan, sailed by Punta Arenas, an important port at the Strait of Magellan which also happens to be Chile's southernmost city.**

Opposite: **The snow-capped peak of Volcan Putana dominates the landscape of San Pedro de Atacama.**

THE ANDES AND ALTITUDE SICKNESS

The single geographic feature that unifies the diverse regions of Chile is the Andean mountain range. Some of the Chilean peaks are taller than the highest mountains in Europe, Africa and North America. The Ojos del Salada, for instance, is 22,539 feet high.

Mountain sickness or *soroche* as it is called in Chile, can occur at altitudes of 10,000 feet, and is completely unpredictable in its choice of victims. Trekkers who have never had altitude sickness before can suddenly come down with it. When it strikes, it is rarely fatal, but often extremely uncomfortable. Victims complain of a sudden lack of coordination, headaches, shortness of breath, stomach upset, and a kind of drunk feeling. This occurs because the air at high altitudes contains less oxygen.

The people who live at high altitudes have adapted physiologically to their environment: their lungs are oversized, they have more blood in their systems, and their hearts are some 20% larger!

The best cure for altitude sickness in extreme cases is descending to a lower altitude. In mild cases, the victim simply rests for three or four days until his or her circulatory system can adjust. In Peru, Bolivia and Ecuador, the customary cure for *soroche* is a tea made from coca leaves.

CHILE'S ISLANDS OF ADVENTURE

The Juan Fernández Islands, 450 miles west of Santiago, and Easter Island, 2,000 miles from Santiago in the South Pacific, are part of Chile. Both territories have interesting histories.

The major island in the Juan Fernández group is known as Robinson Crusoe Island because the real Crusoe, a Scottish sailor named Alexander Selkirk, was stranded there in 1704. Daniel Defoe modeled his hero after Selkirk, but set his novel thousands of miles away in the Caribbean.

Mystery surrounds these stone statues at Easter Island, where there are 600 of them.

Selkirk actually marooned himself on the Juan Fernández Islands after arguing with his captain. Goats became Selkirk's major source of nourishment, as he disliked seafood. He captured goats by outrunning them and tackling them to the ground. When rescued four years later, he could barely speak English and was dressed in goat hides. He became quite a celebrity when he reached London, but said, "I shall never be so happy as when I was not worth a farthing." He even tried to build a cave behind his father's house in Scotland just like the one he lived in on the island. He left for the sea again in 1717, but died from a fever aboard ship in 1723.

Easter Island is one of the world's most isolated islands and has an ancient and mysterious history. Acquired by Chile in 1888, Easter Island has about 2,000 inhabitants, some of them Polynesian, who call the island by its original name, Rapa Nui. The island contains some 600 carved human-like figures that date as far back as A.D. 900. The heads on the statues are elongated, the eyebrows and chins protrude, and the mouths are small. Many of the ear lobes are distended and have carved ear ornaments. Some figures are only 7 feet high, while the tallest is about 70 feet. Even the smaller statues weigh many tons.

How these weighty figures were carved and transported to sites around the island and why they were shaped as they were continues to be a mystery, although many theories have been presented. Experts agree that the statues were originally used as religious idols, and later as burial places. It is estimated that it would take two carving teams working in shifts around the clock about 12 months to carve an average-sized statue.

Robinson Crusoe Island has little in common with the island of Daniel Defoe's book. What they do share is the marooned hero who had no contact with humans for a few years.

Llareta, part of the scanty vegetation of the northern Andes in the Atacama region, is collected for fuel.

CLIMATE

Chile is located south of the equator, so the seasons are reversed. December and January are the warmest months, and July and August are the coldest! Due to its stringbean length, Chile has many climatic regions.

The Atacama Desert in the north is one of the driest places on earth—in many parts there is a shower only once a decade. The average annual temperature in Arica, near the Peruvian border, is a surprisingly cool 69° in January and 57° in July, due to the Humboldt Current which moderates the temperature. Days are often hot and nights extremely cool. Rain falls along the coast and in the Andes.

Santiago, in the Central Valley, has a very stable, pleasant climate. Temperatures average 84° in summer and seldom get as low as 32° in winter. The average annual rainfall in the capital is 14 inches, about the same as in Athens and Madrid. Mornings are often chilly, but never frigid, and the days are rarely so hot as to be called oppressive.

Moving south, temperatures drop and rainfall increases. In Valdivia, the average temperature is 53°, and the average annual rainfall 98 inches. Strong winds blow all year round. Chiloé Island is almost always misty. In the southernmost town of Punta Arenas the average temperature is 43°. Some places have an average rainfall of 216 inches a year. There is little seasonal change in these regions. In some areas of Chile, the bad weather is so unrelenting that places have names like Hill of Anguish, Ice Water Valley and Last Hope Sound.

Pink Chilean flamingos.

FLORA AND FAUNA

Plant life in the Atacama Desert is virtually non-existent due to lack of rain. At higher altitudes, certain species of cactus have managed to grow by absorbing water from the fog that occasionally blankets the peaks. The "candle-holder" (candelabrum) cactus is found at 6,000 feet. It grows less than an inch a year and flowers only once, for 24 hours.

Animal life in the Atacama is equally scarce. A desert seagull called the gray gull is known to nest in the desert, in an area where temperatures surpass 120° during the day. One parent flies to the coast to search for food while the other actually shields the chick from the scorching sun by standing over it to provide shade. Both parent and chick are said to pant like dogs during the hottest part of the day, before the afternoon breezes from the coast sweep across the sand and the desert cools off.

Guanacos, the small llamas of Chile.

At higher altitudes, alpaca, vicuñas, llamas and pink flamingos can be found. Llamas, alpacas and vicuñas are members of the camel family and have been prevalent in South America for two to three million years. Now, all have been domesticated and cannot live apart from humans, who keep them for their milk, meat and coats. Wool from these animals can be made into handsome garments.

The rich soil of the Central Valley is perfect for growing cereal, fruit and grapes. Common trees here include the palm, poplar, weeping willow and eucalyptus. South of Concepción, almost half the land is covered by forests. Chile's national flower, a member of the rose family called the copihue, grows wild in Temuco from October to July. Its colors range from bright red to soft pink to snowy white. The araucaria or monkey puzzle tree, an evergreen, grows south of the Bío-Bío River. Its high quality wood is free of knots, making it ideal for carving.

In the southern regions of Patagonia and Magallanes, birds such as the condor (whose wingspan can reach 17 feet), the black-necked swan, the wild goose, the flamingo and the penguin can be found. Pumas, red foxes and guanacos (small, timid llamas) are plentiful.

An almond orchard. The rich soil and mild climate of the Central Valley is ideal for growing cash crops.

The pudú or dwarf deer lives in the rainforests of South Chile. Measuring only 15 inches tall and weighing less than 25 pounds when full grown, the pudú is the world's smallest deer. A one-week-old baby can sit comfortably in one hand. Pudús resemble tiny antelopes with fox-like faces and spotted coats. They are solitary and tend to travel alone. All day and night they dart in and out of the dense forest undergrowth, snacking on leaves and berries and taking short rests. At one time, pudús were common in parts of the Chilean and Argentinean Andes. Now, their numbers are scarce and they are considered a "vulnerable" species.

Chile's fauna includes some 200 species of fish from the Pacific Ocean that can be found along Chile's west coast. From the northern coast come tuna, swordfish, sole, smelt, sardine, red and black conger eel (a national culinary specialty), octopus, clam, crab, mussels and abalone. Lobster and shrimp can be found off the central coast and salmon and trout can be found in Chile's rivers and lakes.

HISTORY

SOUTH AMERICA WAS POPULATED some 20,000 years ago after Indians crossed the land between Siberia and America. The Amerindians came to Chile about 10,000 years ago. They were hunters and gatherers until 1500 B.C., when they began to farm corn and made permanent villages.

Archeologists know something about Chile's primitive inhabitants because many mummies and tools have been dug up in sites near Arica, the northernmost port. Some of the mummies are more than 7,800 years old. Their tools indicate that they were expert fishermen and used intricate nets and harpoons to catch their food. Many of the men were deaf from diving for shellfish and the women had an unusual arthritis of the neck from carrying heavy loads. A high-protein diet gave them strong teeth.

In Patagonia, Southern Chile, scientists have unearthed the remains of a giant ground sloth. When standing, it was 10 feet tall. It had the body of a rhinoceros, 3-inch-long claws and a bulging head. In North America, sloths became extinct about 11,000 years ago; the Chilean specimen indicates that they existed in South America as recently as 5,000 years ago and may have been hunted by native Indians.

Thousand-year-old mummies, members of the Atacameño tribe, have been found in the Atacama Desert. Their geoglyphs (large rock drawings) can still be seen in the desert. In 1954, goldminers stumbled across the perfectly preserved, 500-year-old body of an Incan boy in the Andes. Scientists have determined that the boy was probably of noble birth, because he was buried wearing silver jewelry, and that he was sacrificed to the sun god during an annual festival.

Opposite: **A Chinchorro mummy displayed in a museum in Chile.**

Below: **Some geolyphs are more than 150 feet high and depict people, dogs, eagles, condors and vicuñas.**

"...this land is such that there is none better in the world."

— Valdivia, in a letter to his Spanish king, writing of Chile.

SPANISH CONQUEST

In the early 1400s, the Incas from Peru came across Chile's northern desert and took the northern half of what is now the Central Valley. Their attempts to claim more territory in the south were foiled by the Araucanians or Mapuche Indians who resisted the invaders with great ferocity. In the mid-16th century, at the time of the Spanish conquest of Chile (the conquest of the Americas in general had begun when Christopher Columbus discovered the New World in 1492), the country had some one million Indians from several different tribes.

Statue of a Mapuche leader.

Spanish explorer Hernando de Magallanes (or, as he is known in English, Magellan) sailed through what is now called the Magellan Strait in 1520. He was the first European to see the southern region called the Tierra del Fuego. In about 1535, Diego de Almagro came to Chile from Peru in search of gold and silver. He got as far as what is now Santiago and went back. The town of Santiago was officially founded by Spanish explorer Pedro de Valdivia in 1541.

The Mapuche were one of the few tribes in the New World to win repeated battles against the Spanish. Valdivia himself was murdered by the Mapuche in 1554. They were clever warriors: they would steal Spanish horses and use them to raid Spanish towns. The Mapuche men soon gave up farm life and devoted themselves to war.

The Mapuche were a rather primitive people compared with the Peruvian Incas. They did not build cities and had few advanced tools. They lived in simple one-room huts made from wooden poles, straw and animal skins. Their language was sophisticated, however, and they loved sports, especially a game called *chueca*, which is like field hockey. In the mid-17th century, the Indians signed a peace treaty with the Spanish but the Mapuche were not really stopped until the late 19th century.

Before he died, Valdivia divided up much of the arable land in Chile among his soldiers and gave them Indian slaves to farm it. This was called the *encomienda* system. When slavery was outlawed, Indians became tenant farmers or *inquilinos* on large plantations or *haciendas*.

Pedro de Valdivia, the Spanish explorer who founded the city of Santiago, now the capital of Chile.

Each *hacienda* or *fundo* was a society in itself. It had its own store, church and sometimes a school. Indians lived in huts on the estate, kept some livestock, and had small patches of land to grow food for themselves. Ideally, the Indians were supposed to be devoted to the landowners, whom they looked up to as fathers. To cement their loyalty, they participated in rodeos and festivals together. The *fundo* system persisted in Chile until the mid-20th century.

During the colonial period, Chile was run by a governor who answered to the viceroyalty of Peru in Lima. The Spanish authority forbade trade with the other Spanish colonies, and this led to smuggling. Many of the landowners gradually lost their loyalty to Spain, which had little interest in a land with scarce gold and an indomitable tribe of Indians.

THE INDEPENDENCE MOVEMENT

In the early 19th century, Spain had power over land stretching from California in the north to Chile's Cape Horn in the south, and from the Pacific Ocean in the west to the mouth of Venezuela's Orinoco River in the east. Less than 20 years later, her only colonies were Cuba and Puerto Rico.

Independence movements developed all over South America for several reasons. Spanish people born in the New World considered themselves more South American than Spanish, and the Spanish government held the colonies back from economic prosperity by imposing strict trade laws. Chileans were also inspired by the American and French Independence movements.

On September 18, 1810, the Spanish government in Chile was overthrown for the first time. However, it was not until José de San Martín and his army of liberators made their way into Chile through Argentina in 1817 that the final victory was in sight. Claiming that he "came to liberate Chile, not to rule it," San Martín appointed a member of his army, Bernardo O'Higgins, the son of an Irish immigrant, as head

22

Opposite: **A Spanish fort built in 1645.**

Left: **The Declaration of Independence of 1810.**

Below: **The father of Chilean Independence, Bernardo O'Higgins.**

of government. Independence was officially proclaimed on February 12, 1818, although Independence Day is celebrated on September 18.

O'Higgins, who is considered the father of Chilean Independence, was an intellectual interested in making cultural, economic and educational advancements in Chile, even for the poor. He built a library, schools, and lighting and sanitation systems in Santiago. Wealthy landowners, who continued to have a hold on Chilean politics and society, and the Catholic clergy did not approve of O'Higgins, and he was ousted in 1823. He was sent into exile in Peru where he died without ever seeing Chile again.

Civil war began in 1830 and the landowners came out on top. In 1833, they adopted a constitution that benefited themselves and the powerful president they elected.

THE 19TH CENTURY

By the 19th century, Chile had won the War of the Pacific (1879–83) against Peru and Bolivia. It increased the country's territory by a third and gave it possession of the Atacama Desert and its valuable deposits of nitrate, a natural fertilizer. Exportation of nitrate gave Chile an important source of income for 40 years. The mining industry created jobs for a whole new group of people that soon became the middle class.

The statue of Arturo Alessandri Palma, in front of La Moneda, the presidential palace, in the Plaza de la Libertad.

President José Manuel Balmaceda, who took office in 1886, was the first leader to attempt to put some of the country's wealth into the hands of the middle class. The upper class and the British, Chile's important trading partner, disliked Balmaceda's policies for social reform, and he was deposed in 1890. Again, civil war ensued and 10,000 Chileans lost their lives.

MODERN CHILE

In 1920, Arturo Alessandri Palma was elected by the labor and middle classes in another attempt to decrease the power of landowners and narrow the gap between rich and poor. He was ousted by a military takeover in 1924, but returned to power in 1925. He wrote a new constitution that separated Church from State, authorized tax reforms, and ensured freedom of worship and new laws to help the poor. Literate males over 21 were given the right to vote (women's suffrage did not come about until 1940). The 1925 constitution governed politics in Chile until 1973.

The 1930s were marked by worldwide economic crisis and the fall of nitrate prices after the invention of artificial nitrates. Many political parties were created in this period. Despite the turmoil, Chile was considered the most invulnerable democracy in South America. Elections were held regularly and the press had great freedom.

In 1964, the first Christian Democratic candidate in Latin America—Eduardo Frei—was elected to the presidency. He began far-reaching social programs for the poor in housing, education and land redistribution. During his time in office, unemployment and inflation rose.

In 1970, Dr. Salvador Allende Gossens, a Marxist and member of the Socialist Party, was elected by a narrow margin. He took over many of Chile's privately owned industries and banks and redistributed land owned by the upper class. Allende never had the support of the Chilean Congress and he could not maintain the support of most of the Chilean people. During his last years in power, the economy faltered and inflation soared. (In 1973, the inflation rate was more than 300% per year.) There were mass demonstrations against his government, strikes and broad rural unrest due to shortages of food and consumer goods.

A military faction led by General Augusto Pinochet Ugarte bombed the presidential palace in September 1973 and Allende was killed. Although Allende's term was short, he left a permanent mark on the people of Chile for his sincere attempts at social reform. The Pinochet government, as you will see in the next chapter, exacted a heavy cost from the Chileans for their foray into Marxism.

President and social reformist from 1970 to 1973, Salvador Allende Gossens.

GOVERNMENT

CHILE WAS THOUGHT to be one of the most stable democratic nations in South America until the government of President Salvador Allende Gossens was overthrown in 1973. From then until 1989, Chile was ruled by a military government led by a dictator, General Augusto Pinochet Ugarte. The Allende government had placed great emphasis on social programs and the Chilean economy suffered greatly during its administration. Pinochet overthrew Allende's government to purge the country of Marxists and to attempt to revitalize the economy. Only recently has Pinochet stepped down in favor of President Patricio Aylwin, who is presently trying to bring the country back under democratic rule.

Under Pinochet's military government, legislative authority was in the hands of a *junta* made up of the commanders-in-chief of the armed forces and the national police. Pinochet was the chief executive as well as the commander of the army. He chose his cabinet, and his government appointed regional administrators, governors of the provinces, mayors of cities, and rectors of the state universities.

THE "DISAPPEARED"

From 1973 to 1989, Chile was ruled by a most repressive government. Pinochet's opponents were rounded up, placed in concentration camps, tortured or simply killed. Many others were arrested and held against their will while some ten thousand people were banished from the country altogether. The Congress was terminated, the constitution suspended, press freedoms curbed, political parties disallowed and other institutions heavily controlled.

Opposite: **President Patricio Aylwin, elected in 1989.**

Below: **General Pinochet, head of Chile's military government from 1973 to 1989.**

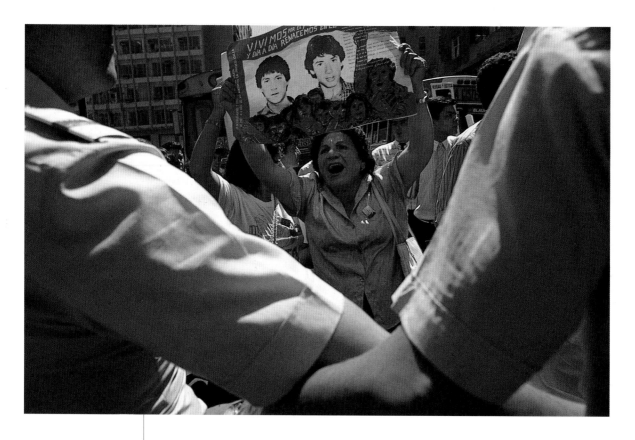

Women demonstrating for the "disappeared."

National police swarmed public squares in Santiago to discourage demonstrations against Pinochet. Protesters were often attacked by trained dogs, fired upon with water cannons or arrested and detained. At times, rigid curfews were set and those caught on the streets after a certain hour were rounded up by the national police.

Books were banned or burned and their authors punished. Pinochet controlled elections and determined when or if they should be held. When they were held, they were often "rigged." People lived in terror of the government and its informers. They were told what to do, what to believe, even what to think. Men were pulled from their beds during the night. Their wives' pleas for information on their whereabouts were ignored. The missing soon became known as the "disappeared."

Rally for Aylwin's party.

RETURN TO DEMOCRACY

In 1988 Pinochet allowed Chileans to decide whether he should remain chief executive for another eight years; 55% of them voted in favor of electing a president. The day after Pinochet's loss, hundreds of thousands of Chileans filled the streets chanting, "*Adíos, General. No vuelva nunca más.*" (Good-bye, General. Never come back again.)

On March 11, 1990, the dictator handed over the presidency to Patricio Aylwin, a member of the Christian Democratic Party. Pinochet planned to remain in command of the army for another eight years.

Aylwin has a very difficult job. A country ruled by terror and repression for 16 years cannot become peacefully democratic overnight. Aylwin has vowed to prosecute those responsible for human rights violations during Pinochet's reign, reinstate press freedoms and political parties, release political prisoners, and allow exiles to return.

PRESIDENT PATRICIO AYLWIN OF CHILE

In 1918, Patricio Aylwin (pronounced "pah-TREE-see-oh AIL-win") was born in the resort town of Viña del Mar. His father was a lawyer and, later, president of the Supreme Court of Chile. His ancestors were from the Basque region of Spain, but his surname is Welsh in origin. His great-grandfather was a British consul in Chile.

Like his father, Aylwin is a lawyer. He was elected to the Senate in 1965 during the government of Eduardo Frei. During Allende's term, he became president of the Christian Democratic Party, and originally supported the military coup. Once he realized that the Pinochet administration intended to use violence to repress the opposition, Aylwin shifted his loyalties and defended the victims of the regime.

Aylwin is considered a moderate who feels very confident of Chile's ability to make the transition to democracy, even though Pinochet will retain a position of power. His stated priorities include convicting those responsible for human rights crimes, maintaining economic stability, and narrowing the gap between rich and poor.

Aylwin is married, has five children and eleven grandchildren, and his family often accompanies him to political activities. He considers Sunday a day of rest, always appears in public in a suit and tie, likes to take a nap after lunch and to eat his meals at home (like most Chileans).

FACTS AND FIGURES

Chile is officially classified as a republic. It is headed by a chief executive, the president, who is elected for an 8-year, non-renewable term. The president lives in Santiago, in La Moneda, the presidential palace. The president appoints cabinet ministers.

The legislative branch of the government, centered in the city of Valparaíso, 75 miles from Santiago, is made up of two houses, the Senate and the Chamber of Deputies. Senators are elected for 8-year terms, and Deputies for 4-year terms. Before the coup, there were 45 Senators and 147 Deputies. About one-third of the Senate is appointed, not elected.

The Supreme Court is the high court of the judicial branch of government. Supreme Court judges are appointed for life by the chief executive. Chile's 11 courts of appeal consist of judges appointed by the president from a list made up by Supreme Court judges. Similarly, judges of lower courts are chosen by the president from a list compiled by judges of the courts of appeal. During Pinochet's rule, a separate military tribunal was organized to try opponents of the regime. This has since been abolished.

There are 12 regions in Chile and the Santiago metropolitan region. These are administered by what are called "intendants," appointed by the president. The regions are further divided into provinces, which are administered by governors. Currently, there are 51 provinces, which are divided into municipalities administered by mayors. During the last administration, Pinochet supporters were placed in positions of power at the national, regional and local levels. Under the Aylwin administration, this may change.

The presidential palace in Santiago, which Pinochet bombed in 1973, killing President Allende.

ECONOMY

CHILE HAS ONE of the healthiest economies in the Southern Hemisphere. In the late 1980s, the unemployment rate was under 8% (comparable to the rate in the United States), the growth rate was 6.5% and the inflation rate was under 15% (compared to 100% in Mexico and more than 300% in Brazil). The Pinochet government, for all its human rights abuses, brought Chile back on solid economic footing.

Much of Chile's success can be attributed to increased exports of Chilean goods. In 1973, 208 Chilean companies exported 412 products to 60 countries; in 1988, 6,000 companies exported 1,400 products to 120 countries. Exports include fresh fruit, fish, copper and wood products. The United States is Chile's primary trading partner, especially in fruit exports. Because Chile is south of the equator, it can put summer fruit like grapes and berries on North American tables in winter. The increase in exports has led to the creation of many jobs for Chile's laborers.

The new wealth created during Pinochet's reign went mostly into the hands of those who were already well off. Out of Chile's 12.5 million people, an estimated 5 million can be considered "poor;" about 1 million live without electricity or water. In cities, some of the poorest, called *los marginados* or the "marginal ones," have had to create their own jobs to survive. They hawk cheap goods in the streets, clean car windshields and beg, or search the city for used newspapers, bottles or boxes.

Yet, though the number of poor in Chile is high, other Latin American nations have many more hungry, homeless people than Chile does. Most Chileans have an increased standard of living since the Pinochet regime. More own television sets, cars, their own homes, many hold shares in private companies and nearly 3 million have joined pension plans, which are quite rare in Latin America. President Aylwin hopes to maintain the high growth rate, but also to introduce social programs to aid the poor.

Opposite: **the copper works at Chuquicamata, Chile's most important copper mine.**

TWO LITTLE GRAPES

The Chilean grape export business made international headlines in March 1989 when cyanide was found in grapes shipped to the United States. The food scare began when the U.S. Food and Drug Administration (FDA) received telephone threats that grape shipments had been poisoned with cyanide. Suddenly the entire fruit export business came to a halt: shipments were impounded in all U.S., Canadian, Japanese and West German ports and some 100,000 Chilean fruit workers were without work. In the end, officials found harmless amounts of cyanide in just two red grapes.

Although most Americans soon forgot the incident, many Chileans still have not recovered. Angry Chilean politicians, farmers and exporters claim that the U.S. government should pay some $333 million in damages to compensate for the losses they incurred.

"The damage is much more than $333 million," said Chilean Senator Sergio Romero, "because this involves the dignity of a country and the prestige of the fruit, on which you cannot put a price."

FACTS AND FIGURES

The per capita income in Chile is about $1,465, higher than that of Brazil, Argentina and Mexico. This represents a 9% increase over the 1973 level. The GDP (Gross Domestic Product) in 1987 was $18.4 billion. Agriculture made up 10% of GDP that year; major products included wheat, potatoes, corn, sugar beets, onions, beans, fruit and livestock. Industry—textiles, metal manufacturing, food processing, pulp, paper, and wood products—represented 21% of GDP in 1987.

Chile exported $5.2 billion in goods including copper, molybdenum, iron ore, fishmeal, fruit, wine, and forestry products to the United States, Japan, Germany and Brazil, among others. Chile imported about $4.4 billion of petroleum, machinery, vehicles, electronic equipment and other consumer goods from the United States, Germany, Brazil, Argentina and Japan.

In 1989, Chile exported approximately 32% of its GDP, an unparalleled rate in Latin America. In 1973, the year the military government took over, Chilean fish exports were $22 million; in 1989 they were $720 million. Similarly, in 1973, fruit exports were $14 million; in 1989 they were $580 million.

An industrial workshop in Santiago.

MINING

Minerals are a very significant source of revenue for Chile. In 1987, they made up 50% of the country's total exports. Copper is Chile's single most important source of wealth. Chile has about 20% of the world's copper reserves and has been the world's largest producer of copper since 1982. The most important mine, Chuquicamata (see page 32), is two miles long, half a mile wide and 1,000 feet deep.

Chile also produces other minerals such as molybdenum, iron ore, manganese, lead, gold, silver, zinc, sulfur and nitrates, once a major source of revenue. The Atacama Desert has the world's largest natural nitrate deposits and almost 33% of the world's metallic lithium reserves.

About 42% of Chile's petroleum needs are met by its reserves in the Magellan Strait, on the island of Tierra del Fuego and in the province of Magallanes. Coal is mined in the Gulf of Arauco region south of Concepción, Valdivia, Magallanes and near Punta Arenas.

Opposite: **Sulfur ore in the Atacama Desert. In the background is Volcano Tocopuri.**

Below: **Wood is processed for manufacture in the Lake District in Chile.**

MANUFACTURING AND INDUSTRY

Chilean manufacturers of paper, textiles, food products, beverages, tobacco and appliances have been affected by harsh economic conditions like inflation, recession and increased foreign competition. Manufacturing accounted for 25% of GDP in 1970, but only 21% in 1987.

Approximately 75% of manufacturing jobs are located in the cities of Santiago, Valparaíso and Concepción. About 12% of the work force is in manufacturing.

A fish packing factory.

AGRICULTURE

Most of the farming in Chile takes place in the 600-mile long Central Valley. Primary crops include wheat, corn, grapes (for wine and the table), beans, sugar beets and fruit. Livestock production is primarily made up of beef and poultry and accounts for about 33% of the country's output. Sheep are raised on farms in the southern regions of the country.

The agricultural industry employs about 20% of the labor force. Many Chileans are migrant farmers who move from farm to farm picking whatever crops are in season.

FORESTRY AND FISHING

Chile is ranked among the top ten fishing nations in the world. In Latin America, it is second only to Peru. Most fishing is done off the northern coast of the country where the primary catch is anchovy, sardine and mackerel. Chileans consume about 93% of the fish catch and export a great deal of canned fish products as well as fresh fish.

Chile has more than a million acres of pine tree plantations, mostly in the Central Valley. Most of the lumber is used to make pulp and paper products.

Harvesting the crop.

Right: **Vats of wine being matured for the table.**

Below: **Chile's grape-growing district.**

CHILE'S WINE INDUSTRY

The fertile lands a three-hour drive south of Santiago are one of the most exciting wine regions in the world. Stretching from Aconcagua Province through Colchagua Province and south to the towns of Sagrada Familia, Lontué and Molina, the wine country is ideal in terms of climate, irrigation, soil quality and the absence of harmful insects.

Vines were originally planted in Chile in the 1500s to make wine for the sacrament of the Catholic Mass. In the mid-1850s, a Chilean wine-grower employed a French wine specialist to grow the grapes that make fine wines. In the 1860s, a blight struck the European vineyards, wiping out most of the crop for many years. The only top quality vineyards that remained untouched were those in Chile. By 1889, Chilean wines were winning important prizes in Paris.

Today, Chile is the largest exporter of wines in Latin America, exporting to more than 50 countries, including Japan, the United States, Canada, Great Britain, Colombia, Venezuela, Argentina and Brazil. Wine has steadily increased its role in the Chilean economy in terms of export revenue and jobs. In 1980, exports were approximately $21.5 million and some 400,000 people were employed in the wine industry.

Chilean wine-makers use European methods. They ferment the grapes in vats. White wine is aged 1–1$^1/_2$ years, while red is bottled after 2–2$^1/_2$ years. The best red wines are aged twice as long. Most Chileans drink the cheap simple varieties sold in grocery stores and labeled *tinto* (red) or *blanco* (white). Experts have remarked that Chilean wines are one of the best bargains in terms of both quality and price.

THE CHILEAN WORK DAY

Just as in North America, the typical Chilean work day is from 9 a.m. to 5 p.m., although people in business often work until 7 or 8 p.m. Chileans are among the few Latin Americans who do not take long lunch hours followed by traditional siestas or naps. Shops are usually open only half a day on Saturday and everything is closed on Sunday.

In general, Chilean businessmen and women are conservative. They dislike aggression and are known to be very trustworthy and honorable when making deals. Women are taken seriously in the job world and need not be aggressive to have their opinions heard. Decisions are often made by only the top management, who tend to be of European extraction. Chileans like an introductory session where they get to know their customer before discussing business. Typical topics of conversation include the family, leisure activities like fishing or skiing, and Chilean wines.

At the stock market in Santiago.

CHILEANS

CHILE HAS MORE than 12.5 million people. The largest group of 66% are *mestizos*, or people of mixed European (mostly Spanish) and Amerindian blood. The second largest group (25%) is European, and the smallest group (5%) is native Indian, mostly from the Mapuche tribe. The remaining people, including the Polynesians of Easter Island, are from various racial backgrounds.

Chileans are sensitive about the subject of racial mixture, even though most have some Indian blood. In general, they are far more influenced by European or North American culture than by the early Indian culture, and they see themselves as Caucasian.

Chileans are not as racially diverse as the people of other Latin American countries. In fact, Chile is said to be one of the most homogeneous countries in the area. Immigrants did not settle in Chile in great numbers the way they did in Brazil and Argentina, and Chile's unique, protective geography has kept it rather isolated from the rest of the world. Small groups of German, French, Italian and Swiss immigrants did come to Chile in the mid-1800s, however. People from England, Ireland, Yugoslavia and Lebanon migrated to Chile in later years. Some typical non-Spanish Chilean surnames are Edwards, Lyon, Schmidt, Newman, Ross and Etienne.

Middle Chile has only 18% of the nation's land, but about 77% of its people. Today, more than 80% of Chileans live in urban areas, compared to only 68% in 1960 and 20% a hundred years ago.

Opposite and below: **Young and old Chileans of the sparsely populated northern region.**

Of these, 40% reside in Santiago, the capital. The next five most populous cities are Viña del Mar, Valparaíso, Concepción, Talcahuano (all in Middle Chile) and Antofagasta (near the Atacama Desert). Most *mestizos* and Europeans live in the Central Valley. Many German immigrants settled in the southern cities of Valdivia, Llanquihue and Osorno. Most Yugoslavs make their home in the Tierra del Fuego, and the Mapuche Indians live mainly in the southern Central Valley near the city of Temuco.

The birth rate in Chile—1.7% per year—is lower than in most other Latin American countries and compares favorably with industrialized countries in the West. The infant mortality rate is comparatively low. About 4% of children die before their first birthday, compared to 13% in Bolivia, 9% in Peru and 8% in Brazil. The average life expectancy is 71 years, compared to 51 years in Bolivia, 64 in Brazil and 58 in Peru. Major causes of death are heart disease and cancer.

Population Distribution in Chile:

Persons per square mile

- nearly uninhabited
- under 3
- 3–25
- 25–50
- over 50

MESTIZOS

Mestizos make up the fundamental ethnic group in Chile. When Valdivia came to Chile he brought only one Spanish woman, his mistress, so his troops married the native Indian women. Within 50 years, the *mestizo* population was higher than the European population. In colonial times, *mestizos* could be found at all levels of society and the same is true today, although they make up a majority of the urban and rural working class.

THE IMMIGRANTS

After the Spanish colonists, the Basques from the Pyrenees were the first significant immigrants to Chile. Arriving in the late 18th and early 19th centuries, they soon took jobs as merchants and traders and bought up large amounts of land. After two or three generations, they were firmly ensconced in the upper class. English, Irish and Scottish immigrants followed the Basques.

In the mid-1800s, thousands of Germans migrated to Chile as part of a Chilean program to populate the country south of the Bío-Bío River. They found the climate similar to that of their German homeland, built German-style homes and became farmers. Now, many Germans raise cattle for milk and grow crops such as potatoes, beets and oats. German names, language, hotels and pastry shops are common in this area of the country.

During the height of European immigration, between 1883 and 1901, only 36,000 Europeans came to Chile. (More came to the United States in a single month during this same period.) Although their numbers were small, the immigrants made a significant impact on society. They had been members of the educated middle class in their native countries and brought much-needed job skills to their new home.

Two of Chile's immigrant population driving a herd down a country road that winds through the fertile Central Valley.

The 25,000 Slavs who migrated to Chile in the late 19th century came to take advantage of the gold rush in the Tierra del Fuego. From there, many became successful fishermen, merchants and shipbuilders. Today, many are professionals, government servants, and businessmen.

In this century, the most significant immigrants were Lebanese. Most established small businesses that later became quite successful (especially businesses for textile manufacturing). Some Jews from Europe and the Middle East also came to Chile. They often moved to urban areas and started retail businesses.

In Pinochet's reign, as many as 1 million Chileans—mostly professionals, intellectuals and artists—left Chile for Argentina, Peru, Mexico, the United States and Panama, among other places. In Pinochet's later years, he allowed many exiles to return. Since the democratic government took control, many Chileans are finding their way back to their homeland.

The Chilean air force recruits from all social levels of the population. Women play a responsible role in the country's defense and politics.

An Aymara Indian at a religious festival in northern Chile.

THE AMERINDIANS

The Chilean Indian population was never particularly large in number or concentrated in one area. The Atacameño and Diaguita tribes lived in the Atacama region; the Mapuche in the area south of the Central Valley; and the Ona and Yahgan tribes in the far south regions. None of the tribes thrived in the presence of Europeans. In 1960, the census reported only 100 Yahgans and 21,500 Atacameños, Quechuas and Aymaras (the last two having migrated from Peru and Bolivia). The Ona and Diaguita had been completely wiped out.

Today, there are only about 400,000 Mapuche Indians in Chile. Also known as Araucanians, the Mapuches fought the European settlers well into the late 19th century. They were the only Indians in North and South America to effectively resist the Spanish during the entire colonial period. It is said that they never really surrendered—they simply stopped fighting.

Valdivia described the Mapuche as strong, handsome, friendly people who were fair in color. Other colonists wrote of their serious manner, their ability to withstand severe hardships and their intimacy with the land they farmed. They did not build temples, for they had no organized religion. They believed in magic and omens sent by trees, birds or the wind. The women were said to be very beautiful in their brightly-colored clothes and beaded bracelets, anklets, necklaces and headdresses. The men were fierce warriors.

Mapuche means "'people of the land" and members of the tribe feel very strongly about the loss of their territory. They separate themselves from outsiders, whom they call *huincas*. *Huincas* are wealthy landowners who, according to the Mapuche, do not look after their own people in times of need.

The Mapuche are a tight-knit group. They speak Spanish when they have to, but prefer speaking their own language. Mapuche feel they have been treated unfairly by the Chilean government, which has given them inadequate portions of land to farm.

On the whole, they are impoverished, have inadequate medical care and few opportunities for advancement. Some 50% of Mapuche infants die before their first birthday. Most live in the country south of the Bío-Bío River, but due to economic hardships, about 25% have migrated to large cities like Santiago, Concepción and Temuco.

Painting of Mapuche Indians carrying off women during a raid on the Spanish colonists. Note their weapon, the *bolas*.

49

CLASS STRUCTURE

In Chile, the class structure resembles a pyramid: the small upper class or elite is at the top; the growing middle class is in the center; and the masses of the lower class are at the bottom. The three classes have vastly different values, ways of life and income levels.

THE ELITE UPPER CLASS Mostly people of European descent, this class includes those related to Spanish colonists as well as European immigrants who came to Chile in the 19th and early 20th centuries. Children of English, Italian, Irish and German immigrants have, for the most part, lost their languages and become wholly Chilean.

The elite holds most of the country's wealth. In colonial times, the upper class traditionally had a house in Santiago, land just outside the city, and a large country estate or *hacienda*. In the post-colonial era, the *hacienda* was often leased to a farmer who paid rent and kept the house in order for the owner's vacation use. Having a country estate is still a status symbol among the upper class.

Chile's upper class is open to outsiders, especially white immigrants, if sufficiently wealthy, although there is no prejudice against *mestizos* who reach a high socio-economic status. A wealthy immigrant could climb the social ladder by marrying into a good Chilean family and buying land. Their children would buy a trading house, mine or more land and marry into the elite class. The third generation was accepted into the elite and added to the family wealth by going into government. The family then had financial, social and political power in the community.

University students in Valdivia, a German-influenced town in southern Chile.

People at the harbor front in Puerto Montt, in the Lake District.

THE MIDDLE CLASS This consists of Europeans and *mestizos*. A hundred years ago, the middle class was made up of only a small group of merchants and small-scale businessmen. The discovery of nitrate and then copper provided significant employment opportunities for Chileans and started the country's modern labor force. Today, people of the middle class work in commerce, service industries, manufacturing and government service. In general, they are educated and family-oriented.

THE LOWER CLASS Members of this class are also *mestizo*. Their ranks include urban laborers, factory workers, domestics, small farmers, sharecroppers, and copper and coal miners, as well as the many unemployed living in the cities. Lower-class families are tight-knit and traditionally provide aid to members in need of assistance. Often, households are made up of people from several generations, many of whom are forced to work to keep food on the table for the entire family.

DRESS HABITS AND COSTUMES

Most Chileans dress just like North Americans. However, they are never as informal or as formal as the most casual or the most fancy Americans. They do not wear shorts to do errands on weekends and they do not wear full-length dresses or tuxedos to weddings. Shorts are usually worn only during the day in beach resort towns. Most people wear nice jeans to go shopping. Men wear conservative suits—not sports jackets—for social or business occasions. Women wear suits and high heels for business and dresses to dine at restaurants or in people's homes. On the most formal occasions, men wear dark suits and ties and women wear cocktail dresses.

Appropriately dressed for a folk festival, with clever use of strong colors.

The most traditional Chilean costume is that worn by the *huaso*, or horseman, during a festival or rodeo, Chile's national sport. He wears a flat-brimmed, flat-topped hat (this originated in Andalusian Spain) and a bolero jacket covered with a waist-length, brilliantly colored *manta* or poncho. The colors of the *manta* are often the colors of the Chilean flag (red, white and blue) or the national flower, the copihue. He wears fringed leather leggings and short, pointed, high-heel boots with spurs. In the 18th century, Chilean spurs were known for their size and decorative quality. They were about 6 inches across and had up to 24 points. Today, the typical spur is only 3 or 4 inches across.

TRADITIONAL COSTUMES OF CHILE

Chilean rodeo performer in traditional flat-brimmed hat of black or brown, and the *manta*, a short version of the poncho. It features an ivy leaf design.

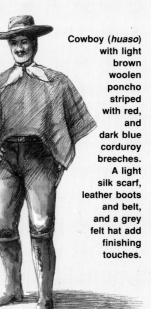

Cowboy (*huaso*) with light brown woolen poncho striped with red, and dark blue corduroy breeches. A light silk scarf, leather boots and belt, and a grey felt hat add finishing touches.

This Mapuche woman shows the influence of Incan culture: a large silver brooch (the *tupu*), silver earrings and headpiece. Her red woolen top and handwoven dark blue woolen blanket skirt are considered modern. Wooden clogs with leather straps make up her footwear.

Chilean rancher in handwoven woolen poncho and a straw sombrero, leather boots and decorative spurs. The spurs are not used to rake the horse's flesh but are pressed flat against the animal's sides. The saddle consists of several layers of felt.

Mapuche Indian on horseback. Beneath the woolen blanket poncho he wears a shirt and trousers of guanaco (llama) wool simply wrapped around the legs and pulled up under the belt. A black felt hat protects his head. A superb horseman, he has no need for such extras as boots, stirrups or spurs. A felt saddle and a simple loop for the big toe are sufficient.

LIFESTYLE

CHILEANS ARE FRIENDLY, generous and honest. They are outgoing, warm and good-natured. They have a passion for Europe and for the arts. They appreciate beauty but scorn ostentatiousness. They are serious about education and politics, and are more accepting of new or progressive ideas than their Latin American neighbors. They are highly tolerant of outsiders yet they cherish their own culture. They are polite without being stiff, proud without acting superior, dignified but not at all snobbish.

Family is of utmost importance. Leisure activities and social occasions often center on the family and the family home is thought of as a sacred place. Unlike many other Latin Americans, Chileans open up their homes to foreigners. Guests are made to feel part of the family.

Like most Latin Americans, Chileans like to take their time about things. In Chile, one need never apologize for tardiness. It is customary to arrive 15 minutes late to a small dinner party and 30 minutes late to a large party. It is even acceptable to be 15 minutes late for a business appointment. Businessmen spend a good amount of time in casual conversation before the first meeting with a new client. Typical Chileans dislike forwardness and aggressiveness of any kind. They like to know someone fairly well before discussing personal or sensitive matters.

Opposite: **The Valdivia quayside shows a strong German influence.**

Above: **A typical Chilean family at Sunday lunch. Notice the paintings in the background.**

LIFE IN SANTIAGO

Nearly half of all Chileans live in Santiago, the fourth largest city in South America. It is the home of Chile's very rich and its very poor. Santiago is the cultural and intellectual mecca of the country, the place where trends are set and where things happen. The city center is the location of government buildings, shops, hotels, offices, movie theaters and restaurants. During rush hours, traffic congestion is serious and in the winter months, the smog is so bad that people wear surgical masks.

An affluent neighborhood in Santiago.

In the late 18th century, Santiago had a population of only about 30,000. Nearly 90% of Chileans lived on farms in the countryside. By the early 19th century, the city had 100,000 inhabitants, good roads and railways had been built, and the colonial aristocracy had moved in.

Between 1865 and 1875, the population of the capital increased to 150,000, due to mass migration from the countryside. This trend continued well into the 20th century because of people's inability to find employment in rural areas. The city did not always provide jobs either, although that fact did not deter many migrants.

Originally, migrants were forced to live in slums or tenements. Then they began to build makeshift homes on the unused land just outside the city. These came to be known as *callampas*, or mushrooms, for they were built so rapidly. About 1.5 million *santiaguinos* (residents of Santiago) live in *poblaciónes* (shantytowns), sometimes 20–30 people in a house, eating and sleeping in shifts.

The homeless of Santiago may not have even cardboard and tin huts. Many are exposed to the elements.

The houses are two-room cardboard and tin huts. Few have running water, but many have electricity, because the residents tapped into overhead lines; some have television sets. Water is brought in from streams some distance away. The residents look for work, but many end up hawking wares or doing occasional manual labor like picking grapes.

The Pinochet government tried to alleviate Santiago's acute housing shortage by building low-income housing. Most were four-story structures—there are few highrises in Chile due to the earthquakes—made up of simple apartments with electricity and plumbing facilities. Although some 30,000 units were built in 1987, much still needs to be done.

Santiago's upper-class inhabitants live in large and luxurious apartments or homes in the *barrios altos* (upper-class neighborhoods). Some of the homes are modern, others are in the colonial style, complete with central courtyard and tiled roof. Many have gardens and terraces that provide spectacular views of the city or the nearby Andean mountain range.

In the upper middle class apartment, the kitchen is the domain of the maid or maids who cook and clean for the upper and upper middle class. In many families, the mother rarely visits the kitchen; she plans menus for the family and writes the shopping lists, but does not cook.

Right: **A typical house in southern Chile.**

Below: **A** *ruka*, **the typical Mapuche house.**

RURAL HOUSING

Although many members of the Mapuche tribe live in modern housing, some still live in traditional dwellings called *rukas*, found primarily in farmland near the city of Temuco. The low walls are wooden and the roof is thatched and comes to a peak. There is an earthen floor, often covered with a beautiful handmade rug, a fireplace that serves as both heat source and stovetop, and sacks of food—potatoes and corn—leaning against the walls.

The traditional Chilean rural house has long, dark corridors with large, high-ceilinged rooms leading off them, a large kitchen and nearby stables. Some of the grander homes have their own orchards and even a small vineyard. Tenant farmers usually live in one-room adobe houses.

LIFE IN THE COUNTRY

The typical rural family in Chile probably lives and works on a farm or *fundo* in the country's fertile Central Valley. The average day on the *fundo* begins at dawn, when the family goes to the barn to milk the cows. At about 9 a.m., they sit down to a breakfast of rolls and coffee with fresh milk.

A house on stilts in Choloé, southern Chile.

During the morning, someone will usually deliver a supply of drinking water, as the farm has none of its own. Then, the father might go to the stables to train the horses for an upcoming rodeo while the mother and children go to the market for fresh fruit, vegetables and seafood. At about 2 p.m., the children put on uniforms and go to school. When they return, they do their homework, and then play a game of soccer or dominoes.

On Sundays, the family goes to Mass together. The meal following the Mass is the most elaborate of the week, and is shared by cousins, aunts, uncles and grandparents. After lunch, the children might go horseback riding or spend time reading.

GENDER ROLES

Like most Latin American countries, Chile is a male-dominated society. Men are expected to provide financial security for the family, while women take care of the home and raise the children. When a woman walks down the street with a man, it is assumed that they are a married couple. If a man and woman marry, they are supposed to have children, preferably boys. The children see the father as household ruler and the mother as care-giver. Men are not likely to do domestic chores, even if they are unemployed. At meals, their wives serve them before the rest of the family.

Opposite: **Chileans on their way to work.**

Below: **In the country, as in the city, women make an important contribution to the family income.**

Chilean children have a sense of duty toward their parents. They often live at home until they marry and when they do leave home, they do not go far. They come home on Sundays and important holidays and they maintain a close relationship with their parents throughout their lives. Chilean parents tend to be more protective of their children than North American parents. They are involved in their children's lives and tend to have a greater influence over them. As a result, children in Chile tend to become independent at a later age.

61

International Women's Day rally in Santiago, 1989. Women in Chile are politically awakened and do not hesitate to take on the government when they feel their rights have been infringed.

Chileans are not as rigid in their interpretation of sex roles as other Latin American countries, however. Chilean women from all social classes are employed outside the home, either by necessity or by choice. Most are domestics, but others work as teachers, office workers, social workers and journalists, etc. There are many women professionals as well.

Women in Chile were very active in political activities during the recent period of military rule. They marched in peace rallies carrying signs that said, "We want liberty—we don't want torture!" and subjected themselves to tear gas and water cannons. They organized themselves into protest groups, campaigned for women's rights, established soup kitchens and schools in the shantytowns, and put pressure on the government to provide information on the whereabouts of their family members. One group of women would perform the national dance, the *cueca*, without the required male partner, as a way of bringing attention to the missing loved one and the government that took him away.

THE CHILEAN LIFE CYCLE

The important events in the life of a typical Chilean are performed in the Catholic Church.

WEDDINGS Chileans are not given to flashy displays of wealth—they tend to celebrate important occasions in a modest, dignified manner. Weddings, for instance, are rarely formal affairs. Most Chilean brides do not choose bridesmaids or attendants to walk before them down the aisle. The bride is escorted only by her father, who hands her to the groom as they reach the altar. During the ceremony, which can be a brief, 20-minute service or a full Mass, the parents of the bride stand next to her and the parents of the groom next to him.

Many people have their wedding parties at home or in a small hall near the church. Wine and champagne are served with the wedding dinner, which often consists of a simple meal of meat, rice, salad and cake. Often there is dancing after dinner, and then the couple leaves for the honeymoon, to Viña del Mar, Rio de Janeiro or Buenos Aires. Members of the upper class might go as far as Europe or the United States.

FUNERALS These are also simple events. The body of the deceased is kept at home for a couple of days before the ceremony. During this time, friends and relatives visit to provide comfort to the bereaved and to say prayers. There is often just a brief memorial church service, followed by a short graveside prayer. Few people wear black to funerals in Chile any more, although traditionally, widows were expected to wear dark clothing for several months after the death of her husband.

The most significant rites of passage are baptism, First Communion, marriage and death. Even the Chilean who rarely attends Sunday Mass will follow these traditions.

CHILDHOOD

Chilean girls do not have fancy parties to celebrate their 15th birthday the way girls do in Venezuela, Cuba and Mexico. Children's birthday parties are also quite modest compared to their North American counterparts. There are no hired clowns, musicians, or merry-go-rounds in the backyard. The children dress in nice clothes, eat cake and ice cream and play.

THE EDUCATIONAL SYSTEM

Chileans have a serious commitment to education and their educational system, based on French and German models, is highly regarded among Latin Americans. Getting a good education is an ambition of the lower and middle classes and providing it has been a passion among Chileans dedicated to social reform.

Education is compulsory but many, such as this poor street boy, are not registered for school.

In 1880, urban children were given free, compulsory education and in 1920, the same was done for rural children. Now, children are required to attend eight years of primary school, and can go on to four years of secondary or vocational school and several years of university. Today, approximately 95% of children between the ages of 7 and 12 are enrolled in private religious schools.

The typical primary school curriculum consists of mathematics, Spanish, English, art, science and writing. The optional secondary school course has two curricula: an arts and sciences program to prepare children going to college; and a vocational program to teach job skills.

Chile's universities are esteemed throughout the region. The University of Chile, established in 1738, has campuses in Arica, Talca, Santiago and Temuco. Its student body has traditionally been made up of members of the middle and lower classes, while the private Catholic University in Santiago has been linked to the elite.

Kindergarten school-children on an excursion.

RELIGION

RELIGION IS ANOTHER element of Chilean culture, like language and ethnic heritage, that unites the people. Nearly 90% of Chileans are Roman Catholics. Just under 10% are Protestant, and of these most belong to fundamentalist sects. The Mapuche Indians have their own tribal religion, and the remaining people are Jewish, Moslem, Buddhist or of the Baha'i faith.

Only about 25% of Chilean Catholics attend Mass regularly. Those in the 11–20 age group attend even less frequently. But Chileans consider themselves to be a Catholic people, despite their lack of formal participation in church activities. As one Chilean puts it, "We are born into a Catholic society and we accept it. We may not be regular church-goers, but we do perform the important Catholic rituals like baptism and First Communion."

Young Chileans see going to Mass as both a religious and a social event. About one-third of them attend Catholic schools, where they are immersed in the teachings of the Church. Many say prayers at night before they go to bed.

Chilean adults practice the Catholic notion of helping the less fortunate. In fact, Chile is one of the most socially committed countries in Latin America. The Chilean clergy—made up of about 2,000 priests (half of them foreign) and 5,500 nuns—has a history of social concern and progressive thought. Many clergymen support family-planning programs, believe that matters of divorce should be handled by the courts, and participate actively in programs to help people living in slums.

Opposite and below: **Pre-teen children throughout Chile are very much involved in Catholic ceremonies.**

Above and opposite bottom: **Worship at shrines is commonplace. Chileans may make a pilgrimage to one, as to the Virgin's shrine, or pray at roadside shrines.**

Opposite top: **Youths praying during the papal visit to Santiago in 1987.**

RELIGION AND SOCIAL CLASS

Historically, the urban upper classes and wealthy landowners have been closest to the Church. A study done in the early 1970s indicated that 12–25% of people living in Santiago attended church regularly, compared to 10–12% in the areas north and south of the capital, and only 2–4% of lower-class people.

The working class had neither the time nor the money to learn the teachings of Catholicism through formal education, and they tended to believe that their destinies were already mapped out and were therefore unaffected by faith. They often became attached to one or more saints or believed in the magical powers of inanimate objects. Most lower-class people, however, turned to the Church to perform the important rites of passage: baptism, First Communion, marriage and death.

During the period of military rule in Chile (1973–89), the middle and lower classes drew closer to the Church. This happened because the Church took a firm stand against the government, its tendency toward violence, and its economic policies in favor of the upper classes. The Catholic Church was responsible for establishing and overseeing a broad range of social programs directed at the families of political prisoners and the poor: school lunch programs for 30,000 children of Santiago; vocational training for adults; and assistance to small farmers and to the unemployed.

The Church was not exempt from Pinochet's fist—members of the clergy were unlawfully arrested and some were even exiled—but it gave the military government a force to reckon with.

Above and opposite bottom: **The oldest church in Chile, the Chiu Chiu in San Pedro de Atacama, and its interior.**

CHURCH AND STATE

The 1925 constitution in Chile provided for freedom of religion and gave the Church independence from the State. The distance between them continued to widen during the 1973–89 military period.

In the mid-1970s, Cardinal Raúl Silva Henríquez established an organization called the Vicariate of Solidarity, a group of full-time lawyers and volunteers dedicated to defending the victims of human rights abuses. The organization also provided counseling for victims and their families and set up workshops in which the wives and mothers of the tortured and the "disappeared" could make *arpilleras*, or embroidered tapestries depicting scenes from everyday life, to be sold to the public.

A church in northern Chile, with basic decor, including the obligatory cross and a shrine in the grounds.

CATHOLIC BELIEFS AND TRADITIONS

Roman Catholics differ from other Christians because they believe that the pope is the leader of the Church and that his word is unquestionable. In the Catholic Church, members are supposed to perform several sacraments to reach a state of grace and gain admittance to heaven.

The first sacrament is baptism, in which infants are cleansed of their "original sin." In Chile, children are baptized when they are about two months old. Parents invite close family members to witness the ceremony in church, and friends to celebrate with them at home. Godparents are appointed before the baptism; they promise to raise the children and oversee their religious education in the event of the parents' death.

The child's First Communion takes place in his or her eighth year. The child attends religious school to prepare for First Communion, which is usually a group ceremony. Girls dress in white lace gowns that resemble bridal attire and boys in suits. After the ceremony, the family meets at home for a modest celebration. A second set of godparents is often chosen before the First Communion. Some parents allow children to make the selection themselves.

Being married in church is a sacred religious event. According to Catholic beliefs, marriage allows a couple to have children and should not be broken for any reason.

Receiving last rites is another sacrament. This action, performed by a priest, cleans the soul and allows it to be admitted to heaven. When the priest performs the last rites, he puts olive oil—a symbol of light, strength and life—on the forehead of the dying and asks for forgiveness for sins committed by each of the senses: sight, touch, taste, smell and hearing.

Opposite: **A Catholic child's First Communion is an important milestone in her religious growth.**

First Communion is an important event because it indicates that the child is now able to confess sins and receive the sacrament, a wafer which is said to represent Christ's body.

PROTESTANTS IN CHILE

About 10% of Chileans are Protestants. Pentacostalism, which falls under Protestantism, is a growing movement in South America, especially in Brazil and Chile. Pentacostals believe in expressing themselves during the service, aloud or through body movements.

The world's largest Pentecostal church is the Jotabeche Methodist Pentecostal Church in Santiago. Founded in the early 20th century by Manuel Umaña, the church now has more than 80,000 members, each of whom attends services once a month, due to limited space in the church, which seats 15,000! The service starts with hymns sung by the entire congregation, accompanied by a 1,000-person orchestra of guitars, violins and mandolins. Worshipers sing, rejoice, dance and shout praises to God throughout the service.

Pentecostals are committed to social reform, although they tend to be apolitical. In 1986, for instance, they were involved in helping the Mapuche Indians retain their land.

Other Protestant groups include the Baptists and the Lutherans, whose members are mostly of German ancestry, and the Seventh Day Adventists.

RELIGION OF THE MAPUCHES

The folk religion of the Mapuche Indians of Chile has roots in Incan mythology and Christian teaching. Like Christians, they believe in the existence of a supreme being.

Their God is called Guinechén, which means "master of the land." He is responsible for controlling nature, creating man and animals and heading a pantheon of other gods who represent the sun, the moon, the stars, the earth, the sea and thunder. To the Mapuches, the forces of evil,

Opposite: **A Mapuche holy man near Temuco.**

74

which bring flood, famine and disease, are embodied in Guecufü, who fought unsuccessfully against Guinechén to wipe out the ancestors of the Mapuches.

Mapuches consult a medicine man or *machi* to cure sickness, to save a failing crop or to receive a blessing. The *machi* has direct contact with the supreme being and enters a trance when he communicates with him.

THE MYTHOLOGY OF CHILOE ISLAND

Chiloé Island, a community of fishermen just south of Puerto Montt, is steeped in folkloric tradition, much of it relating to the sea. Many inhabitants of Chiloé believe in Pincoya, a blond princess and the protector of all sea creatures. She is said to live in Lake Huelde on the island, and to dance on the shore when the moon is full. If she dances facing the hills, the fishermen's catch will be good. A phantom ship, called the *Caleuche*, is said to seduce the island's sailors on board, and then to force them to sail forever.

The island is known for its exquisite wooden churches, some held together entirely with wooden pins instead of nails. Some date as far back as the early 1700s.

Church on Chiloé Island.

The Mapuches, like many South American Indian tribes, believe in mythical animals that can perform extraordinary feats. A beast called a *cuero* is a cuttlefish with many sets of eyes. It seizes swimmers, drags them under the surface and eats them. The *camahueto* is a huge seahorse which can destroy ships. Magicians ride on *camahuetos* when they travel. Fear of sorcerers, witches or devils is common among the Mapuches. Diseases are said to be caused by evil spirits that possess the body or by enemies who cast spells.

LANGUAGE

SPANISH IS THE official language of Chile and is spoken by virtually all of its inhabitants. Chile's rather isolated geography, the Spanish heritage of its people and its common language have contributed to the creation of a homogenous society with shared customs and values.

The Mapuche Indians are the largest group of Chileans with a non-Spanish culture and language. Mapuches speak their own language, Araucanian, whenever possible, but speak Spanish as well. The Aymara Indian language is spoken by a small group of people in the north, and the inhabitants of Easter Island speak Pascuense, a Polynesian language, as well as Spanish. Some of the German, Italian, Lebanese, Greek and Yugoslavian immigrants living in Chile speak their native languages at home but Spanish outside the home.

Many Chileans—those who travel extensively, work in international firms, or whose jobs bring them in contact with tourists—speak English, but the vast majority do not. They appreciate foreigners who make an attempt to speak Spanish, no matter how limited their knowledge of the language. They love talking to foreigners and prefer a poor form of communication to none at all.

Opposite: **Newsvendor in Santiago. The common language is Spanish.**

Below: **When graphics are used, language skills are not needed to know what this Valparaíso vendor is selling.**

CHILEAN SPANISH

The average urban Chilean is said to speak Spanish more carefully than the typical Argentine, but not as purely as the urban Peruvian.

The type of Spanish spoken in Chile differs from region to region and from social class to social class. As in all cultures, the educated and upper classes are likely to speak a more refined Spanish than the lower classes.

Throughout Latin America, people who live at high altitudes tend to sound more clipped; they articulate their consonants but tend to drop their vowels. People who live in the lowlands often do just the opposite; they relax their consonants and retain their vowels. Hence, in Chile, the "s" at the end of a word is often dropped, or pronounced like an "h." *Las mamas* sounds like *la mama* and *los hombres* like *loh hombreh*. *Empanada* comes out as *empana'a*.

Whatever their geographic region or social level, Chileans are known for speaking extremely fast. This causes whole sounds or syllables to drop off completely: *hasta luego* ("so long") becomes *'stalugo* and *dedo* ("finger") becomes *deo*. Non-Chileans who speak perfect *Castellano*, the purist form of Spanish from Spain, may have difficulty following Chilean Spanish and vice versa.

A Chilean can pick out another Chilean in a crowd of Spanish-speaking people from other countries by his or her pronunciation, use of slang or speech patterns. Chileans tend to insert the rolled "r" sound before certain words that they wish to emphasize. "Of course" might come out sounding like "*Rrrrrr-claro!*" and "how pretty!" like "*Rrrrrr-que lindo!*" In addition, Chileans love to add the suffix *-ito* or *-ita*, which means "little," to the end of words. Thus, a grown woman named Gloria might be called Glorita by a good friend as a term of affection. Chileans also often use the Italian word for good-bye, *ciao*, instead of the Spanish *adíos*.

BASIC CHILEAN PRONUNCIATION

SOUND/LETTER	PRONUNCIATION
f, k, l, m, p, t, y, ch	as in the English language
a	**a** as in mark
e	**a** as in make or **e** in let
i	**ee** as in meet
o	**o** as in tote or lot
u	**oo** as in toot
y	**ee** as in meet
b	resembles a **v** when placed between vowels
c	**s** as in sink when before **e** or **i**; or like **k** in kite
d	resembles **th** when at the end of a word
g	like **ch** before **e** and **i**; or like **g** in girl
h	silent
j	**ch** as in the Scottish word loch
ll	**y** as in yes
ñ	**ny** as in canyon
qu	**k** as in kite
r	rolled, especially at the beginning of a word
rr	strongly rolled
s	often dropped at the end of a word
v	**b** as in bird
x	**x** as in taxi; or **s** as in sink before a consonant
z	**s** as in sink

Chilean slang words and idioms distinguish them from other Latin Americans. For instance, they often use the phrase "al tiro" (to shoot) when they mean "immediately."

NON-VERBAL COMMUNICATION

Chileans gesticulate when they speak, but not in an aggressive or confrontational manner. In 1985, when Chilean film director Miguel Littín entered Chile disguised as a Uruguayan businessman to make a movie about life under Pinochet, he had to consciously avoid making expressive hand gestures when he spoke, or he would have given himself away.

As with many Latin Americans, Chileans like to touch each other in greeting, but in a dignified manner. Women friends kiss each other on both cheeks (a European custom) when they meet, and sometimes walk arm-in-arm. Men shake hands with both men and women when introduced. Good male friends usually shake hands and pat each other on the back. It is polite to greet, shake hands with and say good-bye to every guest at a small gathering. At large parties, a "hello" is acceptable.

Chileans generally do not stare at people when walking down the street or riding on a bus. They prefer to look straight ahead without making eye contact.

Right: **If a Chilean holds his hands up, palms outward and fingers apart, he means someone is stupid. Clenching the fist and raising it to eye level is a communist sign, and standing with both arms raised is a sign of protest.**

Opposite: **If the hand is free, it is used to add emphasis to the words.**

SPANISH NAMES AND TITLES

Many Chileans follow the Spanish custom of using a double surname. If a man's name is Carlos Rojas Perez, he is called Señor Rojas. Rojas is his father's surname, and Perez is his mother's maiden name. If he marries a woman named Rosa Montalvo Garcia, she becomes Rosa Montalvo de Rojas, and/or Señora de Rojas. Montalvo is her father's name and Garcia, which is now dropped, is her mother's maiden name. The children of Carlos and Rosa will have the surname Rojas Montalvo.

The only title regularly used in Chile, aside from the usual Señor and Señora, is "Doctor," for a physician.

Spanish culture and language are shared by the majority of Chileans. They are preserved and strengthened by a wide range of publications, all in Spanish.

Easter Island, whose Polynesian community once had their own language and script.

THE RONGO-RONGO TABLETS

The ancient people of Easter Island, a small Polynesian territory that belongs to Chile, had their own language and a long-lost native script that resembled Egyptian hieroglyphics. In 1864, a European missionary on the island noticed that many of the locals had wooden boards, called *rongo-rongo* tablets, on the walls of their homes. These were covered in small pictures of plants, animals, geometric shapes and celestial beings that had been carved in rows using sharp stones. Even then, the islanders could not decipher the tablets.

According to legend, there were three different types of tablets: for hymns, for crimes and for historical events. The ancient ruler of the Easter Islanders, Hotu Matua, was supposed to have brought the tablets in the year A.D. 450. Experts have had little luck deciphering the script on the few tablets that still exist on the island. Some believe the characters do not represent an alphabet, because there are too many of them, but tell some sort of story. Others believe that the pictures are not a script at all, but serve as hints to help people remember important verses.

UNIDOS EN LA GLORIA Y EN LA MUERTE

THE ARTS

CHILEANS ARE AN intellectual people who have great respect for education and admiration for the arts. Santiago, considered by Chileans to be the New York or London of South America, is the center of cultural expression. It is the home of the Museum of Pre-Columbian Art, which contains primitive Latin American artifacts; the Fine Arts Museum with its excellent collection of Chilean painting; the Municipal Theater, where Chileans go to see the Ballet de Santiago, the Philharmonic Orchestra and

the opera; and the San Francisco Church and Museum, which contains an impressive collection of colonial religious art and antiques. The urban home of Nobel Prize-winning Chilean poet Pablo Neruda is also in Santiago and open to the public, as is the Cousino Palace, an 1871 mansion filled with European antiques and decorations.

Chilean artists such as surrealist painter Roberto Matta and sculptor Marta Colvin are internationally recognized. The most important Chilean musician has long been pianist Claudio Arrau, one of the finest interpreters of the works of Beethoven. Chilean composers Enrique Soro and Juan Orrego are well known among Latin Americans. The *Nueva Canción* or New Song movement began in Chile in the 1960s and spread to all of Latin America. Led by musician and poet Violeta Parra, her children and others, the movement concerned itself with social protest and labor reform. It was filled with the revolutionary spirit of the time.

Opposite: **Statue in front of the Fine Arts Museum in Santiago, Chile's capital and cultural center.**

Above: **German costume, dance and music are the tradition in Valdivia.**

Youths painting a mural of Allende.

POLITICS AS INSPIRATION

In the last two decades, many of Chile's finest artists—film-makers, poets, novelists, theater directors, fabric artists, musicians and song-writers— have expressed their disapproval of the political situation through their art. During Pinochet's reign, artistic and intellectual life was severely repressed. Hence, many artists chose to leave Chile; others were exiled.

The art created by Chileans abroad during this period is often concerned with the loss of homeland and the tragedy of a people stifled by a repressive government. Those who remained in Chile also expressed their dissatisfaction with the regime by creating "protest art."

MIGUEL LITTIN: CLANDESTINE IN CHILE

Chile's leading film director and Academy Award nominee, Miguel Littín, was permanently exiled from his homeland by General Pinochet in 1973. After living in Mexico and Spain, he returned to Chile in 1985 disguised as a Uruguayan businessman to shoot an undercover film about life under Pinochet. Nobel Prize-winning novelist Gabriel García Márquez told Littín's story in a fascinating, suspense-filled book entitled *Clandestine in Chile, The Adventures of Miguel Littín.*

To enter Chile undetected, Littín had to adopt a whole new persona. He learned to speak with a Uruguayan accent, to change his characteristic laugh and walk. He lost weight, shaved off his beard, colored his hair and gave up his jeans for a stiff business suit. He was so convincing his own mother did not recognize him when he returned home to his village.

While in Chile, Littín and his underground allies directed more than five different film crews working simultaneously at different locations. The result was some 100,000 feet of film—some shot right in the office of General Pinochet—which was ultimately edited into a two-hour feature film. When García Márquez's book was published in Spanish, Pinochet impounded and burned 15,000 copies in Valparaíso.

Márquez, who wrote the book, *Clandestine in Chile, The Adventures of Miguel Littín.*

A mural in Santiago dedicated to Nobel Prize poet, Gabriela Mistral.

LITERATURE

Literature, especially poetry, is the dominant art form in Chile. In the 16th century, Spanish poet Alonso Ercilla y Zúñigo published an epic poem called *La Araucana* about the battles between the Spanish and the Mapuche Indians. This is considered Chile's first major literary work and is widely read and memorized by schoolchildren.

Gabriela Mistral, or *la divina* Gabriela (the divine Gabriela), as she is referred to by Chileans, was born in Vicuña in 1889 and died in 1957. Mistral was the first Latin American to receive a Nobel Prize in literature. In 1945, the judges honored her "for her lyric poetry, which is inspired by powerful emotions and which has made her name a symbol of the idealistic aspirations of the entire Latin American world."

Mistral, whose real name was Lucila Godoy y Alcayaga, was a poor but educated rural schoolteacher who wrote honest, passionate poetry about Monte Grande, the village where she lived, children and the loss of love (her lover killed himself when she was 20). Her poetry is beautiful, compassionate and shows a special love for the common, country people. As a result, Mistral was worshiped by people of all classes. When she died, the Chilean government declared three days of official mourning.

Poet Pablo Neruda, whose real name was Neftalí Reyes Basoalto, received the Nobel Prize for literature in 1971. (It is said that Jean-Paul Sartre refused the prize in the 1960s because he felt Neruda should have won it.) Neruda too was an advocate of the poor but his poetry, unlike Mistral's, is highly political.

A confirmed communist, and the friend and ally of Marxist President Salvador Allende, Neruda composed verse about poverty, hunger and the plight of the factory worker. He died just weeks before Pinochet came to power, and later became a symbol of the artistic freedoms that were lost under the new regime. In recent years, Chileans flocked to the village of Isla Negra, where he lived, to scratch messages of hope into the fence surrounding his cliff-top home. "Always you are present and in the thoughts of the people," said one. Since Neruda's house was opened to the public (one month after the democratic government took power) many exiled poets and intellectuals have visited to pay their respects.

Much of the poetry written in Chile after Neruda's death concerned the political situation at the time. Since many published literary works were censored, a great deal of the poetry written in the 1970s and 1980s was read aloud in cafés or at the meetings of literary groups, or published in makeshift magazines. Two of the leading poets of this period and the present include Juan Luis Martínez and Raúl Zurita.

"Little children's feet,
blue from the cold,
How can they see you and not cover you,
Dear God!"
— Gabriela Mistral

"This night is the same night; it whitens
The same trees; casts similar shadows;
It is as dark, as long, as deep, and as endurable
As any other night. It is true: I do not want her."
— Pablo Neruda

THE NOVEL

While Chilean poets are known for their extraordinary talent and innovation, Chilean novelists have neither received as much international recognition nor developed as distinct a literary voice to separate them from other Latin American writers. Isabel Allende and José Donoso are two exceptions, however.

Isabel Allende, the niece of ousted president Salvador Allende, voluntarily left Pinochet's Chile to live in Venezuela. There, she wrote her first novel, *House of the Spirits*, which became a bestseller in Europe in 1982 and in the United States in 1985.

The novel tells the story of an aristocratic Chilean family ruled by a violent, passionate patriarch and his tender, clairvoyant wife. Based loosely on Allende's own childhood experiences, *House of the Spirits* is characteristic of the 20th century Latin American novel: it is full of vivid, fantastical stories that place magical characters against a backdrop of a politically volatile and violent society. Isabel Allende's *Of Love and Shadow* and *Eva Luna* have both met with critical acclaim.

In Europe and Latin America, Chilean novelist José Donoso is considered by critics to be one of the finest living authors. Translated into many different languages, Donoso's books are about such subjects as the decadence of the elite, aging and sickness, and childhood demons. His novels are strikingly real and magical. His newest work, *The Curfew*, represents a departure from his other well-known books (like *The Obscene Bird of Night* and *House in the Country*), because it deals with politics and the return of an exiled artist to Santiago.

"In Latin America, we value dreams, passions, obsessions, emotions and all that which is very important to our lives has a place in literature—our sense of family, our sense of religion, our superstition, too."
— *Isabel Allende, in an interview in 1985*

WRITERS IN EXILE

Donoso believes that many Latin American novels written in recent years resemble each other because their authors were living in exile while they were written. Isabel Allende was in Venezuela writing about Chile; Gabriel García Márquez was in Mexico writing about Colombia; Mario Vargas Llosa was in Paris writing about Peru; Julio Cortázar was in Paris writing about Buenos Aires; and José Donoso was in both Europe and the United States writing about Chile.

"All of us who lived abroad during that period ... who *chose* to live abroad, have a terrible feeling of guilt. We didn't share in the history of Chile during a very important time," he said. But writing *Curfew*, he added, provided the opportunity to reclaim "the time that has been lost."

"Politics is the air we breathe ... Everything in Chile is ultimately related to politics."
— José Donoso

Isabel Allende, author of the bestselling novel about a Chilean family, *House of the Spirits*.

TODA PERSONA ACUSADA DE DELITO
TIENE DERECHO A QUE SE PRESUMA
SU INOCENCIA

CHILEAN FOLK ART

ARPILLERAS One of the finest expressions of Chilean folk art is the *arpillera*, a wall hanging done on burlap or sackcloth that depicts scenes from everyday life. The pictures are executed using brightly colored embroidery thread and scraps of old material. *Arpilleras* are made in other South American countries like Colombia and Peru, but in Chile they have special political significance. Most are created by a group of 600 women whose husbands were killed or imprisoned during the military regime.

The women sewed to feed their families and to voice their protests. Some *arpilleras* depict protest marches, candlelight vigils for political prisoners, or people voting to put General Pinochet out of office. Others show simple scenes of children going to school or people in church. Several books have been written about Chile's accomplished *arpilleristas*, as they are called, and the beauty and significance of their art is beginning to be internationally recognized.

Other expertly crafted Chilean tapestries are made in Isla Negra, a small coastal village which is also the birthplace of poet Pablo Neruda. These are done by a group of about 50 women who are wives of local farmers and fishermen. Their *arpilleras* are apolitical but depict charming scenes of the quiet countryside, the dramatic coastline, wheat-threshing celebrations or fruit stands. The embroidered picture covers the entire piece of cloth and can take up to one year to create. The tapestry makers belong to a cooperative which furnishes some 900 different colors of yarn and oversees the quality of each piece.

CRAFTS Mapuche Indians of Chile make beautiful handwoven ponchos, blankets and sweaters which they sell in the main market of Temuco. They are also known for their delicately crafted silver jewelry, graceful pottery and well-made musical instruments like pan pipes and drums.

Mapuche women have found a commercial outlet for their beautiful folk art.

Replicas of Diaguito Indian pottery are available in handicraft stores in Chile. The dishes and jugs have an elegant simplicity. They are sparsely decorated with heads of llamas or birds or black-and-white geometric designs over terracotta. Pomaire, a town about 35 miles southwest of Santiago, is known for its hand-molded pottery made from a dark clay scraped from the nearby mountains. It is fired in large, old-fashioned kilns and then sold from the traditional adobe houses that line the town's main street.

THE *CUECA* Most festivals and celebrations in Chile include the national folk dance, the *cueca*. Inspired by the ritual of a rooster stalking a hen, the *cueca* is the dance of courtship.

A man dressed as a *huaso* and a woman in a full skirt, each holding a handkerchief, dance subtly and expressively around each other as musicians play the guitar, the tambourine and the harp, and the crowd claps, shouts and stamps its feet.

Chileans are said to become rowdy and unrestrained when they dance the *cueca*, and their exuberance is infectious. The best *cuecas* are performed on Chiloé Island, in southern Chile.

LEISURE

CHILEANS SPEND a good deal of their spare time with their families. On Sundays in rural areas, families gather to cook and share a large meal together after church Mass. Then, they might play a game of dominoes. In wealthy urban families, weekend leisure time might be spent at the polo club or country club horseback riding, swimming, or playing golf or tennis.

In the winter, they might take ski vacations together at the excellent resorts only an hour or two from Santiago. In the summer, they probably vacation in Viña del Mar. Middle-class families also take beach vacations, and they enjoy camping in the parks and campgrounds of the Andes and the Lake District.

The middle-class *santiaguino* (resident of Santiago) might spend an evening out at one of the city's many restaurants, and then go to a movie. The typical elite class member would host an elegant dinner party, or go to the opera, the theater or the ballet.

On weekends, teenagers raised in upper-class families are likely to congregate at the shopping mall, just as they do in the United States. Parque Arauco, a multi-level shopping center in Santiago filled with boutiques that sell everything from French perfume to Japanese computers, is a meeting place for Chilean teenagers. They go there to hang out in groups and to see who else is hanging out. On Sundays, it is not unusual to see young couples walking hand-in-hand through Santiago's public parks. In springtime, Chileans of all ages and social classes enjoy flying kites in Santiago's parks and empty fields.

Opposite: **Sun, sand and sea with friends make the perfect Chilean vacation.**

Below: **Shopping is fun at any time, but when a concert is part of the program, it increases the pleasure for some.**

SPORTS

Chileans are active participants in the same amateur sports that interest North Americans and Europeans. They play tennis, golf, volleyball, basketball, polo, and rugby; and they enjoy bowling, horseback riding, jogging, snow skiing, fishing, scuba diving and water skiing.

SOCCER As in Peru, Uruguay, Brazil and Argentina, the favorite spectator sport in Chile is soccer, or what is known as *futbol*. Chile hosts major international matches that attract some 80,000 people to Santiago's National Stadium. The finest professional soccer players are likened to national heroes and are instantly recognizable to nearly every Chilean.

Even as far out as the Juan Fernández Islands, soccer has a powerful hold.

In the 1989 election that voted Pinochet out of office, soccer star Carlos Caszely appeared in television commercials with his mother, who had been unlawfully arrested during the Pinochet regime, and encouraged the people to vote against the continuation of the military government. His appearance, according to many Chileans, was instrumental in swaying the vote against Pinochet.

In the country and the city, boys play soccer wherever they can: in the schoolyard, on the streets, in parks, at home. Matches between schools or soccer clubs are very competitive. Twice each year, Chile's two major universities—the University of Chile and Catholic University—compete in front of fiercely loyal crowds.

SNOW SKIING The Andean mountain range close to Santiago and in the far southern provinces provides Chileans with ideal skiing country. The ski season (June to September or October) attracts thousands of South Americans to the country's 14 ski centers.

Portillo, the ski resort about 100 miles north of Santiago, is world famous. This site of the 1966 World Championships is said to have the finest competitive runs. Farellones, 30 miles from Santiago, is another popular resort, especially for short vacations. Resorts farther south, near Punta Arenas, are unique because only here in all South America can skiers see the ocean while making their way down the slopes. Another ski center, Termas de Chillán, has the longest chairlift in South America, some of the best open-slope skiing in the Andes, and natural hot springs for after-ski bathing. Chillán attracts about 25,000 people a year.

Valle Nevado, the newest and most lavish ski resort in Chile, is about 40 miles northeast of Santiago. It even has facilities for heli-skiing, which is a mixture of skiing and hang-gliding.

Skiing in the Lake District. These skiers are dangerously close to the crevasse in the ice-cap around the summit of the active Volcan Villarrica.

WATER SPORTS Chileans love the beach, and many make a pilgrimage to Viña del Mar each year to swim, tan, gamble at the casinos, walk in the famous gardens or eat fresh seafood in one of the restaurants that overlook the ocean. During the peak of the summer season, the streets are filled with people shopping, searching out cafés, and riding in victorias (horse-drawn carriages).

Deep-sea and lake fishing are also popular sports in Chile. In the north, people fish for tuna, bonito, swordfish, shark and marlin; in the south, fishing for trout is quite common. Some of the best fishing in South America is done in the Lake District, about 320 miles south of Santiago. Scuba diving, boating and water skiing are popular in many areas off the coast.

Jet skis at Pucon. Chile's long coastline encourages a variety of water fun.

KITE FLYING   In the 18th century, Catholic monks brought the first kites to Chile and kite flying became an amusement of the upper classes. Today, *santiaguinos* from all walks of life—laborers, teachers, doctors—fly kites for fun and sport from September (the beginning of spring) until the weather turns cold again. Chilean kites are sold for about 12 cents at small stalls set up on Santiago's street corners.

Thousands of Santiago residents turn out each weekend to fly their kites in public parks. The sky is so dense with kites, in fact, that it is difficult to tell whose is whose. Many strings become intertwined, one cuts the other and sends the kite falling into trees and power lines.

Serious kite fliers belong to clubs like the Chilean Kite Fliers Association, which is divided into teams. In one type of competition, two five-member teams battle to snap the strings of all the opponents' kites. Kites dart across the sky, twirling, jumping and diving to avoid their rivals. The string must be of white cotton, but it is sharpened by a coat of glue and glass powder. Kite fliers often tape their fingers to protect them against cuts. Sometimes, two men handle one kite: one controls its movement and the other lets out string from the 1,000-yard spool.

Kites have been honored in Chilean literature as a national treasure, and to some, they are as much a part of the country's folklore as the rodeo, the *cueca* and the *empanada*, a Chilean snack.

The Chilean rodeo is a popular spectator sport because of its colorful costumes and fine horsemanship.

THE RODEO

Chilean rodeo, which has little in common with the American sport of the same name, has its roots in 16th century colonial society and is a much-loved leisure activity today. It began when Spanish ranchers hosted annual cattle roundups in Santiago to show off their cattle leading skills. Over time, the sport developed into a contest of great skill and horsemanship with very specific rules.

Originally, the teams of riders that competed were made up of landowners and employees; now they are partners or friends, usually members of the middle class, who are often neither ranchers nor farmers. The rodeo teams today often travel from village to village with their families and stay in each other's homes. Women have no place in the competition, but this may be changing.

The Rodeo

Also known as *la fiesta huasa*, the rodeo takes place in many towns throughout central and southern Chile in arenas called *media lunas* or half moons. The competition begins when pairs of *huasos* enter the rings in pursuit of a young bull. The riders are attired in traditional *huaso* dress—flat-topped hats, colorful, short-cropped ponchos or *mantas*, fringed leggings and pointed, high-heeled boots complete with spurs— and their horses are saddled and bridled in festive gear.

The riders attempt to control the steer's movements by taking up positions at the flank and behind it. The aim is to force the steer to stop, without a lasso, at a certain place in the fence. The judges award points according to where the horse touches the bull: no points are given for a block on the neck, two for the shoulder blade, three for behind the shoulder blade and four for the back legs, the most difficult place for the horse to make a block. This action is done a total of three times on each of three bulls, with the riders changing positions each time.

Although the Chilean form of rodeo might sound a bit unexciting to the fan of American bronco-busting, it is actually quite entertaining to the average Chilean, who appreciates fine horsemanship. Occasionally, riders do have a brush with danger, when for instance, they run into a frightened 800-pound bull.

Before the rodeo, it is customary to gather in a large shed outside the *media luna* to eat *empanadas* and drink good Chilean wine. After the event, the crowd cheers the winning riders, who receive only trophies or certificates—no money—as prizes. Then they gather round as the *huaso* dances the *cueca* with the rodeo queen and sings a *tonada*, a touching, sentimental song (similar to an American country music ballad) about a lost love or a sad event.

Chileans come to the rodeo to observe a dignified sport that is significant to their history, and to partake in the festivities that precede and follow the event.

FESTIVALS

THE MOST COLORFUL festivals in Chile are religious. They consist of a procession, a special Mass, and often a market for local crafts and produce. In the Andean countries, folk dances are an important part of the festival. These often have a combination of Spanish and Indian elements.

Patron saints' days are celebrated with small processions in which villagers carry images of the saint through the streets. In Antofagasta, the image of the patron saint of fishermen, San Pedro, is taken out in a boat to the breakwater to bless the first catch of the day. On the festival of The Lady of Carmel, schoolchildren, government officials, members of sports clubs and other devotees pay homage to the patron lady of Chile.

In the past, Chileans were less likely to put on lavish religious celebrations than other Latin Americans. During the Pinochet regime, however, festivals began attracting great numbers of people. Most political gatherings were prohibited during the regime, so holidays offered people the chance to meet their countrymen, and to show loyalty to the church.

Celebrations honoring St. Isidore (patron saint of peasants in northern Chile worshiped in exchange for rainfall and a plentiful harvest), the Lady of Lo Vazquez (worshiped near Valparaíso) and St. Sebastian have been especially popular. Aside from providing community solidarity, holidays and festivals in Chile are important family occasions.

Opposite: **Young rider at Cuasimodo, a traditional festival that occurs a week after Easter.**

OFFICIAL HOLIDAYS IN CHILE

Jan 1	New Year's Day	Sep 18	Independence Day
Apr	Holy (Easter) Week	Sep 19	Armed Forces Day
May 1	Labor Day	Oct 12	Columbus Day
May 21	Navy Day	Nov 1	All Saints' Day
Aug 15	Assumption of the Virgin	Dec 8	Immaculate Conception
		Dec 25	Christmas Day

Right and below: **The Sunday after Easter in Chile is a special time, when Chileans celebrate the festival of Cuasimodo. There are many special events, including horseriding contests (right) and theme costume parades (below).**

EASTER IN THE CHILEAN COUNTRYSIDE

A religious tradition unique to Chile is upheld in villages throughout Central Chile on the Sunday after Easter. Called Domingo de Cuasimodo (taken from a Latin phrase used during the Easter service that refers to Christ's resurrection), the festival is celebrated with great fanfare: houses are decorated, and members of the procession wear costumes and parade through the village on horseback, holding pennants and images of Christ. Families save for a year to decorate the carriages and floats they ride in during the procession. Horsemen don their finest *huaso* dress and drape their mounts in beautiful capes that resemble those worn by the horses of knights in the Middle Ages.

The festival has a fascinating history. In the 19th century, after Independence, groups of bandits who still favored Spanish rule terrorized rural communities outside Chile's larger cities. Outlaws like the Pincheira brothers, who ruled over territory south of Santiago, scared away even government troops. They would steal

valuables from farmers, and sacred objects like gold cups and costly vestments from priests traveling to their various parishes.

To protect the priests, armed *huasos* began to escort them on their travels. In brightly colored riding outfits they would ride furiously through the countryside ahead of the procession, holding an image of Christ and daring the thieves to challenge them.

After the bandits were stopped, the festivity became a religious tradition as well as a chance to show off one's finest *huaso* garb. Today, ranchers and farmers "run the Cuasimodo" dressed in short jackets covered by colorful cloaks, tight black trousers, fancy boots and flat-topped hats. The costume is Spanish in origin, but the reckless riding style is reminiscent of the Mapuche Indians who became expert horsemen in their battles against the Spaniards.

Riders escort priests who ride in decorated coaches. As they parade through the villages, the elderly and the sick come to doors and windows of their houses to receive the sacrament. Men, women and children follow the lead coach in horsedrawn coaches, floats or, in towns where horses are not as readily available, on bicycles or motorcycles.

CHILEAN INDEPENDENCE DAY

Independence Day is celebrated in grand style in Chile. On September 18, Chileans usually spend the day eating meat turnovers called *empanadas* and drinking red wine and *chicha*, a fermented grape drink. On the 19th, the armed forces stage a large parade attended by the president and other officials in Santiago. Smaller parades are held throughout the country.

After the parades, many people gather to perform the Chilean folk dance called the *cueca*. In rural communities, men dress up as *huasos* and women wear full calico skirts to dance the *cueca*. In the cities, regular clothes are worn, but throughout Chile, *cueca* dancers carry handkerchiefs. The dance symbolizes the ritual of courtship. The handkerchief is waved provocatively by both dancers, who are accompanied by folk instruments like the guitar, tambourine and harp. The music intensifies with dancers' movements and the crowd claps and encourages the pair. Independence Day celebrations are sometimes followed by a traditional Chilean rodeo.

Log splitting contests are part of a Chiloé Island festival.

Easter Island ladies during the festival of Corpus Christi.

THE FESTIVAL OF LA TIRANA

Some 150,000 people gather in the village of La Tirana near the Atacama Desert to show devotion to the Virgin Mary each July. Many are members of dance and music clubs that come to honor the Virgin or to give their thanks for favors she has granted during the year. The musicians play trumpets, trombones, cymbals and drums in the middle of a group of dancers who dance for three days straight, pausing only to eat and change their costumes and fantastic devil masks. The dancers say that they need neither stimulants nor alcohol to keep going, that their faith spurs them on. After the dances end, they make a pilgrimage to the church of the Virgen del Carmen.

The village of La Tirana, which means "The Tyrant," got its name when an Indian princess, after being converted to Catholicism, became a tyrant in her efforts to convert the rest of her tribe. Her tribesmen murdered her for her disloyalty, but a priest later succeeded in converting them all. A sanctuary was built to honor the princess and the Virgin. People have come to pray there ever since.

The old man of Christmas comes to the Plaza de Armas in Santiago with reindeer, sleigh, heavy red robe—and a beach umbrella to protect him from Chile's summer, which is at its height in December.

CHRISTMAS IN CHILE

There are two major differences between Christmas in Chile and Christmas in North America. In Chile, it arrives in the middle of summer and is, therefore, not associated with snowflakes, snowmen and snow-laden evergreens. In addition, Christmas in Chile, and in much of Latin America, is more of a religious holiday than a commercial one. Although the large department stores decorate their windows and Christmas trees, and presents and Santa Claus (called *Viejo Pascuero* or "old man of Christmas") are common, the emphasis is still on the story of the birth of Christ.

Christmas in Chile

In about mid-December, many religious families set up nativity scenes in their homes. Some are very simple, with only small images of Joseph, Mary, the Christ Child and a cow, while others are elaborate scenes that show the countryside, the Three Wise Men, the angels, the shepherds and more animals. Some even occupy whole rooms and include such props as grass, lakes and rivers, roads, hills and tiny villagers. In upper-class families, the figures may be made of the finest materials and might have been passed down through the generations. In the poorer families where the figures might have been made from clay or cardboard, the Christ figure is often porcelain. In Viña del Mar, famous full-scale nativity scenes are often set up in public places.

On Christmas Eve, Chileans attend a midnight Mass and have a special holiday dinner. Instead of turkey and stuffing, they often eat lobsters from the Juan Fernández Islands. Some go to restaurants where they indulge in an unusual Mapuche specialty called *curanto*. This dish is made by digging a deep pit in the sand, lining it with herbs, leaves and hot stones, and then filling it with layers of eggs, vegetables, seafood, meats, poultry and pork. More hot stones are placed on the top layer and the pit is covered tightly. Entire wheelbarrows of the dish are served to people seated outdoors at long picnic tables.

An alcoholic drink called *colo de mono* or "monkey's tail" is traditionally made during the Christmas season. It contains a powerful alcohol called *aguardiente*, coffee, milk, sugar, cinnamon and egg yolk. A dry cake or bread called *pan de pasque* or "bread of Christmas" is also a Chilean Christmas tradition.

Since Christmas Eve is full of late-night fun, Christmas Day is often a quiet, family day. Presents are exchanged and relatives visit.

Christmas in Chile is different in many respects from Christmas in North America. It comes in summer, the eggnog is coffee-flavored, and instead of turkey, Chileans indulge in lobster.

FOOD

THE CENTRAL MARKET in Santiago represents the profusion of delicious, fresh foods available throughout Chile. Fruits like strawberries, raspberries, grapes, melons, bananas, figs, pears, apricots and peaches abound. Vegetables like corn, avocados, squashes, potatoes, aubergines, garlic, carrots, peppers, and beans are plentiful. But most impressive are the seafood stalls. They overflow with an almost infinite variety of fish and shellfish straight from the local waters.

Chile is a seafood-eating rather than a meat-eating country like neighboring Argentina. This is due to the lack of land for grazing cattle and the fact that no city in Chile is far from the sea. Fresh fish is inexpensive, so all Chileans eat it regularly. The icy cold Humboldt Current that flows north from Antarctica into the Pacific waters off Chile provides the country with some of the world's finest and most unusual fish. *Locos* (similar to abalone), *machas* (razor clams), *cholgas* (mussels), *erizos* (sea urchins the size of tennis balls), *camarones* (shrimp), *langostinos* (tiny rock lobsters), and *congrio* (conger eel) are great Chilean favorites.

Chilean cuisine has both Indian and European influences. In fact, the national dish, *porotos granados*, has ingredients that characterize Indian cooking (corn, squash and beans), and distinctly Spanish contributions (onions and garlic). Some of the other popular dishes have much in common with Mexican or South American dishes. No matter what the origin of the cuisine, Chileans accompany their food with excellent wines grown in their own Central Valley vineyards.

CHILEAN SPECIALTIES

POROTOS GRANADOS Loved by Chileans from all social classes, this vegetarian stew is made up of Indian corn, beans and squash and Spanish onions and garlic. The main ingredient, *porotos* or cranberry beans, are grown almost year round in the central region, which has a milder, more stable climate. If fresh cranberry beans are not available, dried cranberry or navy beans are a good substitute. Some eat it topped with a spoonful of *pebre*: hot sauce of onions, vinegar, olive oil, garlic, chili and coriander.

EMPANADAS As prevalent in Chile as hamburgers in the United States, they are simple pastries stuffed with meat, cheese or seafood and small amounts of onion, raisins, chilies, olives, hardboiled egg or spices. They are formed to resemble small, crescent-shaped turnovers with twisted edges, and baked until the crust is lightly browned. Chileans eat *empanadas* as a snack, or the first course of a large meal, often with red wine. Heaps of them are served at celebrations or rodeos.

CONGRIO Conger eel is a gourmet treat in Chile. It is not an eel at all, but a long, nearly boneless, firm-fleshed fish with a small tail. Chileans eat it baked, grilled, fried or stewed. The fish comes in three varieties: black, gold and red (the rarest and tastiest). *Caldillo de congrio*, a soup of conger, tomatoes, potatoes, onions, herbs and spices, is a national dish. It is traditionally stewed in an earthenware pot to seal in the seasoning and give it a hearty flavor.

Opposite: **Curanto**, a rich southern dish traditionally cooked in a pit dug into the ground and covered with hot rocks. Ingredients include beef, pork, chicken, lamb, potatoes, peas, beans, lobsters, mussels, oysters and clams.

Below: **Raw seafood is a delicacy. Here, clams are relished with a squeeze of lemon juice, and buttered rolls. Huge sea urchins are another delicacy—served raw with chopped herbs. The flesh is a shocking bright yellow-orange and tiny crabs attached to them are eaten live.**

ALCOHOLIC BEVERAGES

Chileans, like the French, are great wine drinkers. They have wine at lunch, wine at the cocktail hour, wine with dinner, wine at home, and wine in restaurants. Children drink wine mixed with water, leaving out the water as they grow older. By adulthood, they are wine experts.

Chilean wines, of high quality and very reasonably priced, are a source of national pride. Some of the finest varieties sell for less than $2 a bottle in Chile and only about $5 in the United States. Wine critics liken them to French rather than Californian wines in flavor. The best vineyards are found in the Central Valley, which has what is known as a "Mediterranean climate"—a warm summer, a dry autumn, and a mild, frost-free spring. Bottled wines in Chile are graded according to quality: *gran vino* (good), *vino especial* (better), and *vino reservado* (excellent). Red wine is called *vino tinto*; white wine is *vino blanco*; dry is *seco* and sweet is *dulce*.

Harvesting grapes at a vineyard near Santiago, in the Central Valley.

An extremely popular alcoholic drink in Chile, *pisco*, is also made from grapes. Almost colorless, with a light fragrance, *pisco* does not appear strong, but it is. It can be served by itself, mixed with ginger ale, cola or vermouth, or, in its most loved form, as *pisco sour*—a frothy cocktail made with *pisco*, lemon juice, sugar, ice and beaten egg white.

Chicha, a fermented grape-juice drink that tastes like apple cider, and *aguardiente* ("fire water"), a very potent beverage distilled from grapes, are often served at holiday time. *Chicha* is found at Independence Day celebrations.

OTHER BEVERAGES

Unlike other South American countries like Venezuela and Colombia, Chile is not a coffee-drinking nation. A diner who orders "*café*" will most likely get a cup of hot water and a small jar of instant coffee; coffee made from just-ground beans is expensive. One has to say "*café café*" to get good, brewed coffee or *espresso*. A *café con leche* (coffee with milk) is a single spoonful of coffee and a whole cup of hot milk. In many European and South American countries, the mixture is half milk, half coffee.

Some Chileans prefer traditional tea to coffee, while others drink a herbal infusion called *yerba maté*, made from leaves of a shrub belonging to the holly berry family. Enjoyed primarily by rural people, *yerba maté* is made by mixing the ground, greenish herb with hot water and drinking it through a metal straw attached to a filtered pipe called a *bambilla*. The pipe is passed around and everybody drinks from the same straw. Some *bambillas* are beautifully decorated or even made of silver. The tea is taken in small quantities because of its high caffeine content.

After hard work, there's nothing like a cup of well infused *yerba maté* in the rural kitchen, shared with two equally deserving friends.

EATING OUT IN CHILE

Although Chileans prefer eating at home, they do have a wide range of restaurant choices, at least in the larger cities. Santiago, Valparaíso and Concepción have everything from fine dining establishments to hamburger places, and many typical Chilean restaurants in between. In Santiago, some of the most elegant restaurants are in converted colonial mansions filled with flowers and antiques. Some serve classic French or Spanish food; others have strictly Chilean specialties eaten to the accompaniment of Chilean folk music.

In most cases, the word *restaurante* applies to a place where both food and the service are good. This one is at Angelmo harbor, Puerto Montt.

Bars in Chile serve light snacks and drinks. *Fuentes de soda* (soda fountains) serve soft drinks, fruit juices and beer. Most *pubs* sell only alcoholic beverages, although some have *empanadas* or light sandwiches. *Cafeterías* and *hosterías* are simple restaurants serving everyday food. Steak houses offering food cooked on a charcoal grill are *parilladas*. Some even have small grills at each table. *Confiterías* are cake shops where you can also get coffee and tea. *Snack bars* are fast-food restaurants (a popular chain in Santiago is called Burger Inn, and is recognized by its logo: two cows' heads), and seafood restaurants abound.

Many Chilean restaurants offer a set meal called a *comida corrida* for lunch and dinner. This very economical meal often consists of a hearty soup, a main course of chicken or meat with rice, and dessert, which is often ice cream, rice pudding or cake. Diners throughout Chile have to pay extra if they want vegetables, potatoes or rolls to accompany their meal. In the United States, these items are usually included in the price. Waiters (called *garzón* from the French *garçon* for "boy") expect a 10% tip, at most, for good service.

When dining out in a group, one person will often pay the entire check. The other diners will usually take everybody else out at some other time. Chileans do not split the check; they call this, appropriately, "American treat!"

Ice cream is a popular dessert, in restaurants or from vendors such as this one outside the Central Railway Station in Santiago.

Because having a maid is common among middle and upper-class families, women do not spend time in the kitchen. Many do not shop for groceries, even though they do make out the list. And though the kitchens in Chile often have every modern convenience, they are not decorated for public view as living and dining rooms are, and are often small.

MEALTIMES AND TYPICAL MEALS

Breakfast time in Chile is most often between 7 and 9 a.m. The average breakfast consists of just toast and instant coffee or tea—no cereal. Some people eat larger breakfasts of ham and eggs. Lunch is typically served at about 1 or 1:30 p.m. and goes on until about 3 p.m. It is the largest meal of the day and often consists of a first course of soup or *empanadas*, a main course of seafood, chicken or a meat stew, side dishes such as vegetables or potatoes, and ice cream and fruit for dessert.

Chileans take tea in the European fashion at about 5 or 6 p.m. This is called *onces*, which means "elevenses," after the customary British morning tea break taken at 11 a.m. Tea-time is often just a snack such as a fried egg, or toast and cheese, along with something sweet, and tea or coffee. Like their European models, Chileans dine very late. During the week, dinner is served between 8 and 9 p.m.; on weekends, after 9 p.m. At dinner parties, the meal is often served as late as 10 p.m. Dinner food is similar to lunch food and is followed by coffee or herbal tea. Wine and beer are often served, although women prefer soft drinks.

TABLE AND PARTY ETIQUETTE

Chileans may not be as formal as other Latin Americans, but they do follow certain rules at the table and in social gatherings. When asked to a dinner party, it is appropriate to arrive about 15 minutes late. If asked for cocktails, the guest will probably be asked to stay to dinner as well. The host and hostess will be sent flowers before the event, or given chocolates or whiskey at the party itself. Wine is not a proper gift because it is so plentiful and inexpensive in Chile.

A vegetarian buffet of typical Chilean foods.

At a formal gathering, it is considered rude to eat anything, even typical "finger food," with the hands. At sit-down dinners, guests are often served by maids who place a full plate of food before them. Buffets are also common. Good manners require one to eat a little of everything on the plate, even if one dislikes it. When serving wine to someone near by at a dinner party, the bottle must be held in the right hand.

Maids will most likely clear away the dishes and clean up, so it is improper to offer to help. When the meal is over, it is important to spend time talking and thanking the host and hostess before saying good-bye. Thank-you notes are not necessary in Chile, but a short telephone call is made the day after the party.

CHILE

Antofagasta B1
Argentina B3
Arica B1
Atacama Desert B2

Bolivia B1

Calama B1
Chiloé Is. A4
Chonos Archipelago A4
Cochrane B4
Concepción A3
Copiapo B2
Coquimbo B2

Huasco B2

Iquique B1

Juan Fernández
  Archipelago A3

La Serena B2

Magallanes A5
Magellan Strait B5

Ojos del Salada B2

Pacific Ocean A5
Puerto Montt A4
Punta Arenas B5

Quellon A4

San Pedro de Atacama B1
Santiago B3

Talca B3
Talcahuano A3
Temuco A3
The Andes B4
Tierra del Fuego B5
Tocopilla B1
Tropic of Capricorn A1

Valdivia A3
Valparaíso B3
Viña del Mar B2

───── International Boundary
───── Tropic of Capricorn
▲ Mountain
● Capital
● City

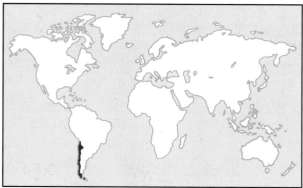

QUICK NOTES

AREA
302,000 square miles

POPULATION
12.7 million

CAPITAL
Santiago

MAJOR CITIES
Valparaíso, Concepción, Viña del Mar, Puerto Montt, Arica

FLAG
(See page 3) The red of the Chilean flag symbolizes blood shed during the Independence struggle, the white symbolizes snow of the Andean mountains, and the blue symbolizes the sky. The white star, a native Indian symbol, also represents Chile's progress and honor. The Chilean flag was designed by a U.S. volunteer in the Chilean army and was adopted in 1817.

NATIONAL FLOWER
Copihue, a member of the rose family.

HIGHEST POINT
Ojos del Salada (22,539 feet)

OFFICIAL LANGUAGE
Spanish

MAJOR RELIGION
Roman Catholic

NATIONAL DANCE
The *cueca*.

CURRENCY
Peso (1 peso = 100 centavos)

MAIN EXPORTS
Copper, fish, wood products, fruit

IMPORTANT ANNIVERSARY
Independence Day (Sep 18)

LEADERS IN POLITICS
Salvador Allende Gossens (1908–73)—first Marxist president of Chile
Patricio Aylwin (1918–)—current head of state, member of the Christian Democratic Party
Bernardo O'Higgins (1778–1842)—first Chilean head of state, and leader of the Independence movement
Augusto Pinochet Ugarte (1915–)—led the military *junta* to overthrow the Allende government; head of state from 1973 to 1989

LEADERS IN LITERATURE
Pablo Neruda (Nobel Prize recipient 1971)
Gabriela Mistral (Nobel Prize recipient 1945)
Isabel Allende
José Donoso

GLOSSARY

cueca   National dance of Chile; resembles a courtship ritual.

empanada   Popular Chilean snack; turnover stuffed with cheese, meat or seafood, and spices.

huaso   Chilean cowboy or horseman.

mestizo   Person of mixed blood; in Chile, often a person of European and Indian heritage.

santiaguino   Inhabitant of Santiago.

BIBLIOGRAPHY

Chile: A Country Study, U.S. Government Printing Office, Washington, D.C., 1982.
Chile and Easter Island, Lonely Planet Publications, Berkeley, CA, 1987.
Chile in Pictures, Lerner Publications Company, Minneapolis, MN, 1988.
Devine, Elizabeth and Braganti, Nancy L.: *A Traveler's Guide to Latin American Customs and Manners*, St. Martin's Press, New York, NY, 1988.
García Márquez, Gabriel: *Clandestine in Chile: The Adventures of Miguel Littín*, Henry Holt and Company, New York, NY, 1986.
Phelan, Nancy: *The Chilean Way: Travels in Chile*, Macmillan, London, 1973.

INDEX

Picture Credits

Victor Englebert, Paz Errazuriz, Robert Francis, Eduardo Gil, Susan Mann, Marcelo Montecino, Tony Perrottet, South American Pictures (Peter Francis and Tony Morrison), UPI/Bettmann Newsphotos